T0064878

ENGLAND IN THE AGE OF CHIVALRY

. . . And Awful Diseases

ENGLAND IN THE AGE OF CHIVALRY

. . . And Awful Diseases

THE HUNDRED YEARS' WAR AND BLACK DEATH

ED WEST

Skyhorse Publishing

Skyhorse Publishing books may be purchased in bulk at special discounts for sales promotion, corporate gifts, fund-raising, or educational purposes. Special editions can also be created to specifications. For details, contact the Special Sales Department, Skyhorse Publishing, 307 West 36th Street, 11th Floor, New York, NY 10018 or info@skyhorsepublishing.com.

Skyhorse® and Skyhorse Publishing® are registered trademarks of Skyhorse Publishing, Inc.®, a Delaware corporation.

Visit our website at www.skyhorsepublishing.com.

10 9 8 7 6 5 4 3 2 1

Library of Congress Cataloging-in-Publication Data is available on file.

Cover design by Rain Saukas

Print ISBN: 978-1-5107-1988-0
Ebook ISBN: 978-1-5107-1993-4

Printed in the United States of America

Contents

Introduction

In February 1308, the king and queen of England were crowned at the newly finished St. Paul's Cathedral in London, a heavily ritualized coronation ceremony that dated back to the time of the Vikings and represented God's anointment of the monarch.

The new queen, Isabella, was the twelve-year-old daughter of France's King Philippe Le Bel, 'the handsome,' and had inherited her father's good looks. With thick blonde hair and large blue, unblinking eyes, she possessed great intelligence and cunning, cruelty as well as compassion, and a skill for hiding her feelings. Her new husband, King Edward II, was a brainless, boneheaded man of twenty-four years whose idea of entertainment was watching court fools fall off tables.

It was a fairy-tale coronation for the young girl. Well, apart from the fact that a plaster wall collapsed, bringing down the high altar and killing a member of the audience. And that the king was gay, and spent the afternoon fondling his lover Piers Gaveston while ignoring the queen.

Edward had put Gaveston, newly created as Earl of Cornwall, in charge of the ceremony, and the king and 'keeper of the realm' sat side by side beneath a coat of arms displayed on the wall, arms not of the new royal couple but the king and earl.[1] After the ceremony,

Edward went and sat with his 'minion' rather than the queen, and the two continued to touch each other throughout.

Gaveston also upstaged Isabella on her special day by wearing flamboyant clothes, according to one eyewitness 'so decked out that he more resembled the god Mars than an ordinary mortal.' The royal favorite was dressed in imperial purple embroidered with pearls, a provocatively regal outfit unsuitable for a courtier from a minor noble family, probably done deliberately to annoy the queen and her relatives. Most insulting of all, Gaveston was wearing the jewels that Isabella's father had given to Edward as his wedding present; the French king's other gifts, including prize warhorses, had also been handed over to his lover. A London chronicler said 'rumors circulated that the king was more in love with this artful and malevolent man than his bride, that truly elegant lady, who is a most beautiful woman.'

And to cap it all off, Gaveston was put in charge of the catering and managed to ruin it all with undercooked chicken. Understandably, the new queen was rather upset by the day's events, while her uncles, Louis and Charles, stormed out of the coronation banquet and returned to France, after 'seeing that the king frequented Piers's couch more than the queen's.'[2] (Visiting England, they must have been prepared for the worst on the culinary front.)

Gaveston also managed to hugely irritate the country's leading barons that day. The Coronation is a heavily symbolic and ancient event that day. dates back to King Edgar in 973, and like the Frankish ceremonies it was based on, it represented divine approval. But for everyone who was anyone, it was also a big party in which they got to show how important they were. Instead, Gaveston was given roles that were traditionally carried out by the great noble families who, it must be remembered, also had their own private armies. He got to carry the crown, as well as the *curtana*, 'the sword of mercy,' which was placed on the altar until redeemed by the king with an offer of gold; and he got to do the fixing of a spur to the king's left foot. That Gaveston landed these roles angered the leading barons so much it began a feud so bitter that after twenty years most of the leading players had been brutally murdered.

Edward and Isabella's marriage, rather unsurprisingly, did not end well; but the uniting of the English and French royal families that resulted from their wedding was a far bigger disaster. King Philippe died in 1314, months after burning to death the leaders of the chivalric order the Knights Templar, whose Grand Master had shouted from the flames a curse on Philippe and his house. His three sons would all die young, none of them leaving male descendants. Only one of Philippe's grandsons would survive to become a king, Isabella's son Edward—and his claim to the French throne would then plunge the two countries into a bitter, horrific conflict that in the Victorian age became known as the Hundred Years' War.

Over the next few decades, France would be devastated by enormous bands of desperados, criminals, and bloodthirsty mercenaries plundering the countryside, to such an extent that large numbers of people took to living in caves. Whole towns were destroyed and their populations murdered. It was the worst war of the European medieval period, but it also marked its end, as the dominance of aristocratic knights was destroyed first by the longbow, and later by firearms.

Historians call this period 'the crisis of the Late Middle Ages' and one reason it appears so grim is that for so long people had finally been having it good—well, relatively. After centuries of chaos and misery traditionally called the 'Dark Ages,' western civilization had in the twelfth century exploded: the first universities were founded, literacy vastly increased, Europe produced great philosophers for the first time in centuries, cathedrals were built, stone houses replaced wood, internal warfare declined, and in most areas of technology Christians equaled the ancients. The 'feudal anarchy' of the eleventh century, a war of everyone against everyone, evolved into increasingly stable and organized central authorities, with Church-sanctioned peace creating the conditions for trade, industry, and art.

The population swelled, as did levels of trade with the continent. Cities like London for the first time reached their Roman-era numbers. A rising population meant a bigger pool of labor and more hungry mouths, before agricultural technology had allowed Europe to escape the Malthusian trap, which is the theory first pointed out by Rev. Thomas Malthus that population growth exceeds food production and so leads to famine. (Agricultural improvements in the past two hundred years have so far disproved this, but until then it was not possible.) The real wage rates of English farm workers, which can be calculated from the early thirteenth century onward, had plunged to their lowest yet. Immense pressure was placed on resources and diet; people were a lot smaller than two centuries earlier, with many suffering from bone diseases and weakened immune systems.

The mild weather of this era, an unusually hot few centuries called the Medieval Warm period, had allowed Europe to produce more food—but now the earth cooled and, as a result, in 1315, the spring after the Templars were burned in Paris, the continent was hit by severe rains and the crops failed. The Great Famine of 1315–1317 killed as many as one in ten people in England, but even this was not the worst thing that happened that century. That dubious honor went instead to the Black Death, the rat-borne disease of the 1340s that ended the lives of between a third and a half of Europe. The population of England, five million in 1300, had fallen to just half that a century later.[3]

Even to those not coughing out plague-ridden black blood, life was unimaginably grim—half of people died before twenty, and life expectancy could be as low as eighteen in some poorer parts of England.[4] Although infancy was the most dangerous time, even those who reached adulthood and lived a relatively long life would have endured various chronic illnesses and pains. Not that 'childhood' in the modern sense really existed; medieval boys worked from age seven and could be hanged at that age. Girls could expect to be pregnant by fourteen, a condition they would endure for much of the next two decades, at a time when one in sixty labors ended in the mother's death. By the time they were thirty they were worn out or, as Geoffrey Chaucer put it, 'winter forage.'

And plague, famine, and war weren't even the only disasters. There was also a split in the Catholic Church between two men claiming to be pope, one a ruthless mass murderer and the other clearly insane, causing much suffering and death. In the middle of the century there was a disastrous banking collapse in Italy, as well as a number of large earthquakes. France and England both saw extremely violent rural uprisings. Everything that could go wrong went wrong, and many writers lamented that the world was coming to an end.

Yet this period also gave us some of the greatest works of art and poetry, by the likes of Giotto, Dante, Boccaccio and, in England, Geoffrey Chaucer. Painting was transformed in this period, so that the king who ended the century, Richard II, is presented in full renaissance glory in the *Wychton Tripdich*, one of England's most famous artworks. The period also saw the most important development in constitutional history, the birth of the House of Commons, and the establishment of Parliament as the lawmaking body on which the monarch depended. It all began with Edward II's terrifying father and his insatiable appetite for war.

CHAPTER ONE

Long Live the King

Edward II had not had the easiest childhood, being the youngest of sixteen children to Eleanor of Castile and the violent maniac Edward Longshanks, confusingly called Edward I even though he was the fourth king of England to be named that.[1]

The first Edward, standing at six foot three, was a domineering, terrifying figure also nicknamed 'the Hammer of the Scots' as well as 'the Leopard,' after a then-common belief that the animal could change its spots, as he had a habit of going back on his word. He was also known as 'the Lawgiver' or 'the English Justinian,' after the Roman emperor, as he introduced laws firmly establishing Parliament, and in particular created the House of Commons, although without really meaning to.[2]

Edward had become king in 1272 after the long reign of his simpleminded father Henry III. Longshanks's grandfather King John had been such a disaster that, after alienating everyone through his lechery, drunken violence, and cowardice, his barons had forced on him a peace treaty that later became known as Magna Carta, which he immediately ignored.[3] Following a year of subsequent civil war, John died of dysentery in late 1216, having gorged himself to death on food and alcohol, and left his nine-year-old son in charge, so broke he could not even afford a crown for his coronation and with his enemies in control of the majority of the country. But, thanks to the heroic elderly knight William Marshal who led the loyalist forces into battle despite being in his seventies, young Henry survived to become one of the longest reigning monarchs in English history.

The essential cause of the conflict had been how much the barons could restrain the king, and who paid for what, and after the First Barons' War of 1215–17 the same problems arose again in the 1250s. The rebel leader this time was a mildly psychotic French knight called Simon de Montfort who led on a platform of low-self-awareness populist xenophobia despite living a fantastically luxurious lifestyle and having only arrived in England in his twenties without speaking a word of English. He was also married to King Henry's sister, and the king was terrified of him.

Henry's eldest son Edward had grown up during this difficult period. Apart from sharing a lazy eye, father and son were nothing alike. Henry was an absentminded simpleton who managed to get lost in the one battle he took part in; his eldest son, named after the eleventh-century saint Edward the Confessor, was a bloodthirsty maniac whose lifelong ambition was to go on a Crusade and bring Jerusalem back to Christianity in an orgy of violence.

Like most young aristocrats, Edward was trained for war through 'tourneys,' or jousts, which had begun in western France in the eleventh century as sort of toleration zones for violence. Although we have in our minds an idea of tournaments as colorful events where men got to show off to women waving handkerchiefs, they were incredibly violent affairs that often ended in multiple fatalities; in 1240 during a tourney outside Dusseldorf, sixty knights were killed in one event. But neither this nor Church condemnation made the slightest bit of difference to the endless supply of aristocratic yobs who loved these events. In June 1256, around the time of his seventeenth birthday, Edward took part in his first tourney at Blyth in Nottinghamshire, at which a number of jousters died from their wounds.

During the early stages of de Montfort's protests, Edward had sided with his uncle, but as it became more violent he returned to his father, and it was Edward who won the war at the battle of Evesham in 1265. It didn't end well for de Montfort: before the battle, Edward assembled a hit squad of a dozen men, the 'strongest and most intrepid at arms' to kill his uncle, who ended up being chopped into a number of parts, and his testicles hung around his nose. (Edward's ally Roger Mortimer struck the killer blow and so his wife got to keep de Montfort's head.)

Many considered Edward's behavior after the battle, when he executed a number of de Montfort supporters, to be murder, but this ruthlessness was characteristic. As a young man, he once ordered his attendants to put out the eyes and crop the ears of an adolescent who angered him. The gossipy monk Matthew Paris tells a story about Longshanks being out with his followers one day when he gratuitously orders the mutilation of one man, just for larks. Such was his reputation that the Archbishop of York had an interview with the king, and afterwards was so shaken he took to his bed and simply died. Another cleric, sent by his fellow priests to complain to the king about taxation, fell down dead on the spot.

Then there was an incident in 1303, when Edward's treasury was burgled and crown jewels stolen; after the culprits were caught, he had the thieves' skin nailed to the treasury door. The royal account book of 1297 includes the cost of repairing his daughter Elizabeth's coronet, which Edward had thrown into the fire in a rage. And, like any great psychotic medieval despot, he was an enthusiastic persecutor of Jews.

Still, Edward was very loving to his pet falcon, and he even used to visit the shrine of Thomas Beckett to offer prayers for his bird, and made a wax image of the sick animal—so not entirely a bad person.

Before becoming king of England, he had been put in charge of Gascony, the region of southwest France still ruled by the English monarch. On one occasion, Edward was dealing with Gascon rebels who had holed up in a church in La Reole, and ordered it destroyed only for his father to overrule him (Henry loved churches). Gascony formed part of the Duchy of Aquitaine, which had become part of the English crown after the ill-fated marriage of Henry II and its heiress Eleanor of Aquitaine in 1152 (it wasn't very happy—he imprisoned her for fifteen years). After their son John had lost most of his French territory in 1204, Gascony remained the last part of the continent attached to the English crown, but the French claimed it. Still, it does produce very good wine so we can see their point, and at the time, Gascony sold five million gallons of the stuff to England every year—some twenty-five million bottles, a large amount when it was very expensive to import.

With England at peace, beginning in1269 Edward took up the gap year of his day, the Crusades. He wanted to do what every young rich kid did: take a year off, experience new cultures, see some really interesting countries, kill all the inhabitants, then go home and bore everyone senseless talking about it. Strangely enough, he brought his wife Eleanor of Castile with him, even though they already had two kids.

The couple had been married since 1254, when they were both children, and were devoted to each other. While on Crusade, Eleanor gave her husband *Concerning Matters Military*,[4] or *De Re Militari*, a book on war by the late Roman writer Vegetius. It was sort of the *How to Win Friends and Influence People* of its time and read by everyone who mattered. The couple had an enduring romantic attachment unusual for the age, and unlike most medieval kings, Edward had no mistresses.[5]

The plan had been to go on joint Crusade with his cousin, King Louis of France. However, the whole adventure was ruined when, after decades of planning, the French at the last minute chose to head to North Africa instead, where Louis soon died (later becoming Saint Louis on rather dubious grounds). Edward ended up first in Tunis and later in Palestine where he fought Sultan Baibars, a Turkish leader who occasionally skinned prisoners alive, according to one chronicler. However, by the time Edward arrived in the Holy Land, the Crusades were as good as lost and, in 1272, he made preparations to return home; before he left, though, he was almost killed in Haifa, in modern-day Israel, at the hands of the Assassins, an Islamic cult led by an enigmatic figure called 'the old man in the mountain' who trained young fanatics to become suicide-killers. An assassin, after securing a private audience with Edward, took out his dagger and stabbed him before Edward overpowered and killed the man; however, the knife was poisoned, and Edward's life was only saved when his wife sucked out the poison. This part of the story sounds slightly unlikely, but its popularity reflected the genuine love match that existed between the two.[6]

This was just one of many amazing scrapes the adventurous king survived, on top of storms at sea, two battles in which he came out unscathed, and a miraculous escape after his horse slipped at Winchelsea, which should have crushed him. Edward was once playing chess and then got up to stretch his legs for no reason, 'only to have a stone crash down from the vaulting in the place where he had been seated,' crushing his chair 'to matchwood.'[7] After this, he became devoted to the shrine of Our Lady at Walsingham in Norfolk, the holiest place in England, convinced that someone up there was looking out for him.

Edward was nowhere near as religious as his father, or credulous; he could easily spot frauds, of which there were many at the time, such as a knight who claimed to have had his blindness cured at the tomb of Henry III and whom the king dismissed as a liar. Henry had devoted years and vast amounts of money to rebuilding Westminster Abbey, originally constructed by his hero Edward the Confessor, but at the end of Longshank's thirty-five-year reign almost no work had been done at the still-unfinished church. He did own a huge number of relics, including a nail from the Cross and a saint's tooth 'effective against lightning and thunder,' but these could be seen more as valuables than any great display of faith.

In 1272, Edward was in Sicily when news reached him that his father had died, and also came news of the death of his son, John, aged just five. When the Sicilian king John of Anjou marveled that he mourned just the former, Edward said he could make another son but fathers were irreplaceable. Edward and Eleanor had sixteen children in total, of whom only four outlived him. The king was a very unsympathetic figure, but life was extremely grim for everyone and there was no room for sentiment.

It was another two years before the king arrived home, like any gap-year kid having come back with huge debts,[8] and on his way back he was invited to a tournament with one thousand English knights in Chalon-sur-Saone in Burgundy. The event turned out to be so violent that the pope himself condemned it, with many of the French *chevaliers* clearly trying to kill the king. He never fought in a tourney after that.

It seems strange for any young man to not even bother to return for his father's funeral, especially when he had inherited the crown of England, but having personally removed the testicles of the last man who had caused trouble, he correctly doubted that anyone else would try their luck. Because the new monarch was so far away, the king's council started a tradition by declaring that the new reign had begun immediately, rather than how previous reigns began when the crown jewels and armory were seized and any rivals thrown out of the nearest window. It is for this reason that the phrase 'the king is dead, long live the king' was invented, and why a half-mast flag was not flown at Buckingham Palace when a royal died again until 1997, when the tradition was changed after the death of Princess Diana.

After the crown was put on Edward's head, he theatrically took it off and said 'he would never take it up again until he had recovered the lands given away by his father to the earls, barons, and knights of England, and to aliens.' This wasn't going to end well.

Chapter Two

The Round Table

Edward's coronation was a lavish affair and the feasting lasted two weeks. One hundred Scottish knights who turned up allowed their horses to run free and declared that anyone who caught one could keep it, and because of this act of reckless generosity the English knights felt the need to do the same. Two years earlier England had experienced famine, the first of many over the next half century, but such lavish flaunting of wealth was common because the entire medieval hierarchy was based on the idea that lords had to be able to entertain those below them. This is what caused kings and barons to ruin themselves and encouraged wars where they would get rich on plunder or die trying. The pinnacle of this idea of kingship was the mythical King Arthur, who, when not winning battles or showing his chivalrous qualities with the ladies, was looking after his improbably large entourage with great feasts and a constant supply of goodies. Arthur was Edward's role model and inspired his desire to become King of Britain, a dream that did much to form the identities of the island's three nations—England, Scotland, and Wales—although this was the opposite of what he intended.

The whole story of Arthur was basically made up by twelfth-century churchman Geoffrey of Monmouth who passed it off as history, and it became immensely popular across Western Europe. The Arthurian legend also fed into the evolving idea of chivalry, which as the medieval period went on became more like its modern ideal, celebrating knights who were brave and dashing but also compassionate and Christian.

The Arthur myth was based on the obscure wars of the Dark Ages between native Britons and invaders from the continent, the Angles and Saxons, who referred to their enemies as 'foreigners,' or *Welsh*; although by Edward's time they had come to refer to themselves as *Cymru*, 'the people' (today the Welsh nationalist party is called Plaid Cymru). Relations between the Welsh and English had never been warm, although the border had been stabilized in the eighth century by King Offa of Mercia, who built a dike to mark it.

Then, however, the Normans turned up, and after conquering England they created a series of semi-independent territories on the border, known as the Marcher Lordships ('march' means border, from where we get such words as marquis, Mercia, and Denmark). The Marcher lords tended to be the toughest and greediest of the Norman aristocrats, which is saying something, and were often in conflict with the monarch. They had also begun to encroach into Wales, grabbing the low-lying fertile land and settling it with English and Flemish migrants.[1] The Welsh, understandably, weren't entirely pleased, but because of its mountainous geography it was impossible to unite the country under one ruler. However, in the 1260s, a strong leader called Llywelyn ap Gruffydd became the first man to be recognized as Prince of Wales; then he refused to turn up to Edward's coronation in the confident belief he could snub him—hence his name, 'Llywelyn the Last.'

Llywelyn was a big fish in a small pond; he had a court large enough to include a bard, a harpist, falconers, and a 'silentiary,' whose job it was to keep the rowdiness to an acceptable level. But he was small-fry compared to Edward, and didn't even control all of Wales, which was divided among him and his three brothers, including Daffyd, who back in 1272 had plotted to assassinate his elder sibling. Forgiven by Llywelyn, he went on to conspire against him on a second occasion, this time with their brother Owain, before a snowstorm forced them to abort and run off to England where Daffyd was sheltered by the king.

As a result, the Welsh prince refused to attend the coronation. Edward demanded he pay his respects, and when Llywelyn again refused, the king of England even traveled up to Chester to save on the Welsh leader's travel expenses. Again, the prince declined, and in total Edward sent Llywelyn five summons, determined to have his way.

The Welshman sent three replies, explaining that he was waiting until their differences were sorted out, namely that Edward hand over the rebels. To add further insult, the fifty-something Llywelyn then married Eleanor, the twenty-three-year-old daughter of Simon de Montfort and Edward's aunt, Princess Eleanor, without the king's permission, and in fact without even having met her. (Strangely, it was possible at the time to marry someone without meeting them so long as an agreed substitute turned up at the wedding). It was this that set off Edward's slightly crazed mission to conquer all of Britain, using the Arthurian fantasy as his justification.

Wales was, for most Englishmen, still a wild and strange place, its people thought to be ruthless and bloodthirsty. In deepest Wales (*pura Wallia*), where the Normans had not settled and where Llywelyn's rule held sway, the old Laws of King Hywel Dda still applied; disputes were settled by blood feuds, and a thief would be pardoned if he had passed ten houses and 'failed to obtain anything to eat' before committing his crime. To the Normans, of course, starvation was no excuse for theft and would inevitably result in some important body part being removed.

In 1276, Edward raised an army and the following year invaded Wales, the English troops advancing under the flag of St. George they had brought back from Crusade; Llywelyn soon surrendered but was allowed to retain the title of Prince of Wales, partly as a sort of mockery to rub in how powerless he was. Edward had kidnapped his cousin Eleanor while she was en route to marry the Welsh leader, but now agreed to the match; however, she died in childbirth, and he had her daughter imprisoned almost from birth in case she might prove a rallying point for rebellion. She lived to her fifties, a captive her entire life, and an illustration of what a lovely man Edward was.

War broke out again in 1282, this time started by Daffyd, after which his elder brother felt obliged to join in an obviously doomed rebellion. The Archbishop of Canterbury tried to meditate, and an offer was made whereby Daffyd had to go on Crusade with Edward while Llywelyn would be given a big estate in England. The Welsh leader gave a romantic response by saying he would not betray his people; romantic, but obviously insane, as they didn't stand a chance. By the end of 1282, all Welsh resistance was over. Llywelyn died on December 11 at the hands of a common English soldier in Powys who had failed to recognize him as a valuable hostage.

Daffyd was soon captured and convicted of treason, murder, sacrilege, and plotting against the king, and his sentence was four corresponding punishments: respectively, dragged by horses, hanged, disemboweled, and quartered. Before he was dead, his intestines were slashed from his body and burned in front of him; his corpse was then sent to various English cities, and his head placed on a spike at the Tower of London, along with his brother's. At the English garrison at Shrewsbury, where Daffyd was killed, a fight broke out between the London and Yorkshire contingent over who got the head, which the Cockneys won. Not the most dignified end, all in all.

In 1284, Edward passed the Statute of Wales, formally ending its independence. To this day, Wales is technically part of England, which is why only England, Scotland, and Ireland are represented on the Union Jack.

There had long been a prophecy among the Britons that the 'lost lands' of England would be recovered and that a Welshman would again one day wear a crown in London. Llywelyn sort of fulfilled that, except it was as a rotting corpse, and the English had stuck a crown of ivy on his head in mockery. His decomposing head remained on a spike at the Tower of London for fifteen years before someone thought to take it down.

The new king cemented his control over Wales by building a series of castles, many of which still stand, among them Caernarfon, Flint, Rhuddlan, Conwy, Criccieth, and Aberystwyth. These could be defended with as few as twenty soldiers and, with stairs that led directly to the sea, withstand a siege for several years. Edward's castles in Wales were inspired by a knight from Savoy with the odd name of Othon de Grandson who had gone on Crusade with Edward and became his right-hand man from the mid-1260s, and these grand monuments were supposed to reflect his claim to be Arthur's heir as ruler of Britain. Edward chose Caernarfon as a site because it was believed that the father of the brutal fourth-century Roman emperor Constantine the Great, one of Edward's heroes, was buried there. (Constantine legalized Christianity but he also killed his own son and wife, along with countless others, so he was not absolutely guaranteed to get into heaven.) Caernarfon became a focus for Edward's megalomania. It was a small village in which he built an enormous castle based on the great city of Constantinople, complete with Roman-style imperial eagles. In fairness to Edward, though, the Welsh tourist industry does pretty well today thanks to his fantastic Arthurian castles.

While in Caernarfon, he claimed to have discovered the body of Emperor Magnus Maximus, who, according to Welsh legend, was the father of Constantine, even though he lived after him, and the grandfather of Arthur who lived three hundred years later. Maximus had supposedly dreamed of a maiden living in a castle and tracked her down and married her, her home supposedly being on the site of the future Caernarfon Castle.

The great Marcher lord, Roger Mortimer, who was Llywelyn's deadly enemy, held the first Arthurian Round Table event at Kenilworth Castle in Warwickshire in 1279. Mortimer's mother was Welsh and he claimed descent from the mythical king. The event featured one hundred knights and one hundred ladies, and at the end Mortimer was presented with barrels which everyone assumed contained wine but were actually full of gold. These Round Tables were sort of sanitized, family-friendly versions of tourneys in which women attended and there was far less bloodshed.

In 1284, Edward accepted the supposed Crown of Arthur—another dubious relic—for an even bigger Round Table feast in north Wales, along with the bones of Maximus. Although the mythical King Arthur, had he existed, would have surely supported the Welsh against the English, the legend increasingly became co-opted to justify the unification of Britain. Edward even had two corpses found a century earlier at Glastonbury Abbey under mysterious circumstances reinterred as 'Arthur and Guinevere.' It is recorded that Edward's Round Table party in north Wales was so popular, with attendees coming from all over the realm, that the floor gave way. Edward may have taken this as a sign of how loved he was, although since the last person who snubbed one of his invitations ended up having his head used as a football, it's hardly surprising that there were no regretful RSVPs.

While in Wales, one of Edward's knights was hit by an arrow fired from a longbow, a native weapon that shot missiles so hard and fast they could penetrate a church door. Edward was so impressed he hired Welsh bowmen to become the core of his army and the longbow would have a revolutionary impact, making the military power of the aristocratic cavalry obsolete.

Welsh tradition held that no man born on foreign soil could be prince, so the king of England swore that the new Prince of Wales would be Welsh-born, and would 'speak no English'—and promptly presented his baby Edward, recently born in Caernarfon.

Apparently, the Welsh lords found this funny. Edward became the first Prince of Wales, and since that day the first son of the monarch has held that title and been crowned in Caernarfon Castle. Sadly, the only problem with this story is that Edward's son did not take the title until he was sixteen, in 1301, although it's true that Longshanks did take his heavily pregnant wife on campaign (strangely, this was quite common). It makes a nice story, but the next king to be crowned Prince of Wales in Caernarfon or anywhere in Wales was Edward Saxe-Coburg-Gotha, the future Edward VIII, in 1911.

The Welsh now found themselves subject to oppressive laws, forbidden to bear arms or even to entertain strangers overnight without permission from the authorities. For the next six hundred years, their language would be discouraged; yet, despite this, still utterly baffling to outsiders, it survives.

The Welsh war had cost a lot of money, and to raise more the king turned on an easier target. The Jews of England had arrived with William the Conqueror, and more came after most of them were burned out of the Norman capital Rouen. The sixteen thousand-strong community was never popular, but Edward lived in a time of increasing religious fanaticism, which had begun to ramp up first with the wars in the Holy Land and then in the thirteenth century with the Albigensian Crusade against the Cathar heresy in the south of France, which cost one million lives. Simon de Montfort had expelled all the Jews from Leicester, while the Church had also become noticeably more intolerant; the 1215 Lateran Council had for the first time insisted that Jews wear special markers on their clothes. Henry III, a credulous man with a double-digit IQ, was the first king to endorse the blood libel, the widely believed conspiracy theory that Jews were ritually murdering Christian boys.

Since Christians were banned from lending money and Jews were banned from doing almost everything else, this became their chosen profession, so that among the most prominent moneylenders were Jews, such as Aaron of Lincoln, Isaac 'the Russian' of

Hampshire, and Belaset of Wallingford, who also lent large amounts to the crown for projects such as Lincoln Cathedral. But this made Jews vulnerable to both embittered debtors and broke rulers.

Edward used a crackdown on counterfeiting as an opportunity to extract thirty-six thousand pounds from the Jewish population, and to execute over two hundred Jewish men on charges of forgery, as well as a number of Christians. In 1274, the king pushed through the Statute of Jewry, which stated: 'Each Jew, after he is seven years old, shall wear a distinguishing mark on his outer garment, in the form of two Tables joined, of yellow felt.' To modern ears this carries a somewhat sinister ring, although rules about clothing were widespread, and it wasn't only heretics, lepers, and prostitutes who had to wear special clothing (the latter were required to wear their clothes inside out) but each social class; in some countries, aristocrats had to wear fur by law, even in the sweltering heat.

After massacres at York and elsewhere by yokels who were enraged about something or other, Edward decreed that 'no [i]nquiries be made,' and in 1282 he began rounding up Jews and demanding payments for their release. Eight years later, he had the rest expelled, ensuring that many were robbed on their way to France and Flanders, and a large number were left to drown in the Thames. All in all, that invitation from Yad Vashem may take a while.

Incredibly, Edward's expulsion of the country's main financiers did not lead to the economic miracle he was hoping for and England's problems continued to get worse. Italians were brought in as replacement merchants, where they set up a banking community in Lombard Street in the City of London—which is still at the heart of the financial sector—not far from Old Jewry.[2] Their terms for the Latin units of currency, *lire, soldi,* and *denari,* from the Roman system, became the *£, s, d* of pre-decimal English currency, and survives as the symbol of the British pound.

The Welsh war of 1277 led Edward to borrow vast amounts from the Ricciardi of Lucca, one of Italy's major banking families, and by 1294 he was in hoc to the tune of four hundred thousand pounds. Always desperate for money, that same year he increased the tax on wool to two pounds a sack but backed down in 1297 after a revolt by leading lords who cited Magna Carta as legal grounds.

His reckless spending did, however, help to create the most important political institution in democratic history. English noblemen had first began having get-togethers they called 'parliament' as far as back as the 1230s, where they would sit around complaining about the king's French in-laws, but under Edward the original group of lords was joined by a second chamber. Longshanks called two 'parliaments' a year because he needed money, and in the 1270s the crown was in such desperate need of cash that it was decided that, because lords could not coerce the realm on their own and the consent of a larger group was needed, a second house of parliament was created, an assembly of knights that later became the House of Commons. (Soon afterwards, representatives of larger towns were invited to sit in the Commons alongside them.) Most of these early members of Parliament (MPs) were knights in the sense we imagine—84 percent of the 854 men in the parliamentary roll of arms in Edward II's reign did military service.

What followed was what many historians call a 'fiscal revolution,' which doesn't sound hugely exciting, but it had a huge impact on our lives. It meant that the Commons were required to vote through any money the king wanted to raise, so by the end of the fourteenth century the lawmaking body was firmly established.

King Edward confirmed parliamentary powers and enshrined Magna Carta into law within it, so his role in later creating English democracy is important, even if he did once threaten to hang a MP who disagreed with him. Most people, however, probably know him better as the bad guy in a classic Mel Gibson action film.

CHAPTER THREE

Braveheart

Wales was relatively easy to defeat, but Edward then got embroiled in the far more complex politics of Scotland, which was another matter altogether. The northern kingdom was at that point absurdly violent, at every level of society. The border with England was inhabited by feuding clans who lived by cattle rustling and whose honor culture fed an unending cycle of revenge killings; considered a nuisance by both countries, many ended up being paid to live in Ulster and then onto the Appalachians. Further north were the even more terrifying Gaelic-speaking Highlanders, viewed as bandits by the lowland Scots, as well as various Viking throwbacks on the islands.

The northern English were terrified of the Scots, and occasionally a horde would pour over the border, attack some villages, and enslave a few locals, before inevitably collapsing into chaos. Then the English would head north with a massive army, burn everything in sight, and the Scots would simply hide until the invaders got hungry or bored.

Many people's knowledge of the Scottish Wars of Independence probably comes from *Braveheart*, a film in which the heroic William Wallace and Robert the Bruce are portrayed as regular fitba[1]-loving Scotsmen who only want freedom, while the English king is a sadistic, aristocratic proto-Nazi and his son an effete homosexual. In reality, Bruce was an Anglo-Norman nobleman who owned several estates in England and France, and like Edward spoke French as a first language (Edward most likely couldn't even speak English). Wallace was basically a criminal psychopath whose penchant for skinning people alive just happened to get caught up with the general violence of the time. Today he probably would have ended up in a high-security correctional facility sporting a tattoo on his eyeball.

Having said that, though *Braveheart* is possibly the most historically inaccurate film since the Messiah wore flares in *Jesus Christ Superstar*, Edward I was essentially your standard Hollywood English bad guy and his son was gay.[2]

Scottish history is complicated because a lot of its identity was made up in the nineteenth century by romantic novelists like Walter Scott and is now used to sell golfing holidays. The Kingdom of Scotland had developed from a merger of four different ethnic groups who, for various reasons, ended up at the edge of Europe; the Gaelic-speaking Scotti in the West, who had migrated from Ireland after the fall of Rome; the indigenous Picts of Caledonia in the North and East, who spoke a mysterious language that mixed Celtic and pre-Celtic words and got their name from their habit of painting their faces; the Britons of the southwest, who were related to the Welsh; and the Angles, who colonized the southeast of the country, which used to be part of the Kingdom of Northumbria. It was because of the Angles that the Scots came to speak a dialect of English, which became dominant after a large influx of English aristocrats following the Norman invasion. On top of this, the islands were also heavily settled by a fifth group, the Vikings, many of whom maintained a Scandinavian identity into quite recent times.

The first Pictish king to use the title King of Alba, or Scotland, was Kenneth MacAlpine in the ninth century, although some argue that accolade should go to his grandson Donald 'the Madman.' The most famous early Scottish monarch was Macbeth, although he was nothing like the Shakespearean character and was actually one of the few kings not to have murdered his predecessor; in the century before he ruled, five Scottish monarchs were assassinated and four were killed in battle. Macbeth, inevitably, went the same way.

England's and Scotland's aristocracies had been interlinked since the Norman conquest, when the remnants of the English royal family moved north and married into the House of Dunkeld. By Edward's time, nine out of thirteen Scottish earls held lands in England, while seven of their English equivalents owned property in Scotland.[3]

Like England, Scotland had a Norman ruling class, although bizarrely the Scots actually invited the Normans over as a sort of imported nobility, which many of those accustomed to the Normans must have regarded as unwise. Most of the Scottish barons, therefore, were basically French, including the great hero of independence Robert the Bruce (or le Brus, if you want to be strictly accurate). Bruce's grandfather had fought with Edward against de Montfort in his capacity as an English lord.

By Edward's time, Scotland had developed from being a very impoverished place—a century before it hadn't even had any cities—although compared to England, let alone France, it was still backwards. Culturally, it had become much more like England, too, and those in the south of the country, Lothian, basically saw themselves as English; they felt far more in common with people across the border, who spoke their language, than with the Gaels to the North. The town of Dryburgh, which today has a statue of William Wallace, was described at the time as being 'in the land of the English as well as the Scots.'

Scotland might well have been absorbed by its larger neighbor in the previous century had it not been for the war between John and the barons, and now Edward saw his chance to make it part of England—however, it only had the opposite effect of helping to create a Scottish identity, as there's nothing like a huge army rampaging through your lands to change how you see your neighbors.

The Wars of Independence began by chance. In 1286, Alexander III, King of Scots, was on his way back to spend his first night with his new young French wife Yolanda, and in his enthusiasm to get home in terrible weather rode his horse off a cliff by the Firth of Forth. His body was discovered in the morning.

Both his sons had already died, as had his daughter Margaret in childbirth, so his only heir was Margaret's two-year-old daughter by King Eric of Norway, another Margaret, called the 'Maid of Norway.' Alexander's first wife—confusingly, yet another Margaret—had been King Edward's sister, and so the ruling families were related. In fact, back in 1284 Alexander was the first to come up with the idea of a union of crowns, and for the Scottish royals the thought of becoming ruler of all Britain and getting to live in London obviously seemed like a great idea. However, in 1290 the then six-year-old Maid of Norway was on her way to her new kingdom when she died of seasickness in the Orkneys (people did actually die of seasickness; sea travel at the time was so dreadful people usually made wills before starting a voyage).

Edward was devastated, not because she was his great-niece, but because it scuppered his plans for her to marry his son Edward and therefore peacefully take over Scotland. It also threw the Scottish crown into chaos, with fourteen different men now claiming the throne.

That same year, King Edward was also slightly unhinged by his own wife's death. Queen Eleanor had been widely disliked for her rapaciousness, making a fortune cheaply by buying debt-ridden estates, and was 'high-handed and ruthless,' as one contemporary complained. She ended up very rich, so as the words to one popular song went: 'The king would like to get our gold/The queen, our manors fair, to hold.' And while most queens tended to bring out the merciful side of their men, she encouraged her husband to be more severe.[4] The chronicler of Dunstable Priory could only say of Eleanor upon her death that she was 'A Spaniard by birth' who had 'acquired many fine manors.' Which doesn't exactly suggest she was a national treasure.

For all his genuine grief, Edward turned his wife's death into something of a PR exercise, and had a cross built at every stop her body rested for its journey from Lincoln to London, twelve in total, and three of these Eleanor Crosses still survive.[5]

Meanwhile, the Scottish situation was getting incredibly confusing. As there were so many possible claimants to the throne, Edward insisted he be head of the selection process, an inquiry called 'the Great Cause,' which comprised eighty Scots and twenty-four Englishmen.

The two main contenders were John Balliol and Robert the Bruce, both great-great-great-grandsons of a previous king, David I. Balliol had the best claim, as his grandmother was the elder sister of Bruce's, and he was also essentially English, his father being lord of Barnard Castle in County Durham; this helped him in Edward's eyes, since Longshanks's main aim had been to 'reduce the king and kingdom of Scotland to his authority,' as he put it.

However, the inquiry ended up taking two years, prolonged after a third, sort of joke candidate entered, Floris of Holland (who Edward later had murdered for an unrelated reason). The whole thing went on so long that they had to have three adjournments before Edward chose Balliol on condition he recognize him as his overlord—a puppet. Balliol did not even dare call himself king in Edward's presence but 'your man of the realm of Scotland.'

Longshanks argued that English monarchs took precedent over Scottish ones because, according to Geoffrey Monmouth's fantastic account of early Britain, the country had been first inhabited by Trojans from modern-day Turkey, and the eldest son had founded modern-day England while the younger had settled to the North. Even at the time, the argument sounded rather tortured, and his real case was that he was strong and they were weak, and he had enormous catapults and they didn't. The Scots royal family were supposedly descended from Scota, a warrior princess daughter of a Pharaoh who captured the country from the family of Brutus—'Citation needed,' as a Wikipedia editor might put it.

Then in 1295, the French invaded Gascony and it all exploded again.

Relations between England and France had been stable for many years because Henry III and Louis IX had been married to two sisters. While Louis died on Crusade in 1270, his son Philippe III also enjoyed a good relationship with his cousin Edward I. He was called the Bold despite being famously indecisive, but, in 1285, he also passed away and was replaced by his son Philippe IV, or *Le Bel*, who was extremely ambitious as well as good-looking: 'The handsomest man in the world, [he] can do nothing but stare at men,' said one chronicler. This was because he was shy, I should add.

Philippe did see eye to eye with Edward on one thing—he expelled all the Jews from his country, too. Otherwise, though, they didn't really get on, as Philippe had his eyes on Gascony, and the two kings had previously argued. Back in 1291, Edward was supposed to arrange the marriage of his son Edward to Blanche, the king of France's sister. However, after hearing how beautiful she was he decided he wanted to marry her himself, so he sent his brother Edmund to sort it out. Philippe went back on the deal and Blanche was married off to a German while Longshanks instead got her younger sister Margaret. He was about sixty, she was maybe seventeen, and Edward was hugely excited about marrying the young French woman; her thoughts on the matter were not recorded but no doubt she was delighted.

Then, in 1294, while Balliol was being set up by Edward as his stooge, Philippe summoned the English king to do homage as his vassal for Gascony, a deliberately humiliating act. Edward dispatched his brother instead, and so in 1295 the French invaded Gascony and also raided Dover. Edward ranted: 'the king of France, not satisfied with the treacherous invasion of Gascony, has prepared a mighty fleet and army, for the purpose of invading England and wiping the English tongue from the face of the earth.'

As a puppet, John Balliol had proposed a tax on the Scots to pay for the English to fight the French, which obviously went down like a lead balloon. The Scottish Council of Nobles furiously rejected Edward's demand for military help. Instead, Balliol began a very ineffective uprising against England, before quickly backing down again.

The English king marched north and besieged Berwick just inside Scotland, demanding the town's surrender; the locals bared their buttocks at him, which considering they had very meager defenses, was not a good idea. The king was busy knighting some soldiers when the English navy began to attack and so he was forced to start the battle early. Afterwards, he massacred several hundred of the eleven thousand population, but in an act of woolly liberalism, he allowed the garrison of two hundred to surrender, expelled the remaining population, and burned down the city. Either soon before or soon after, depending on who you believe, the Scots raided nearby Corbridge and slaughtered two hundred English civilians.

Edward had Berwick rebuilt, wheeling the first barrow of earth himself, true to his gritty image. He enjoyed the all-round toughness of soldiering and would sleep out in the cold with the troops on campaign when, in December 1294, now a grizzled fifty-five-year-old, he besieged Conwy in north Wales and found himself cut off by floods, the king divided up his wine with his soldiers and refused to have more than his share of rations.

After marching into Scotland, Edward took to London the Stone of Scone, the traditional rock of Scottish kingship that was supposed to have been brought from Ireland by the first Scots kings, and he installed another puppet ruler in Balliol's place. Edward judged Balliol as in contempt of court and sentenced him to lose three castles and towns: 'Like a lamb amongst wolves,' one contemporary described him.

Edward now went on a tour of Scotland, getting as far as Elgin, which was further than any English king had ever been. The difficult part, however, was not in defeating the Scots but in running the place, the governor of Scotland being an especially unsought-after job. The Earl of Surrey, the man who Edward had forced to administer the country, was in a matter of months desperately trying to palm it off to others. He spent most of his time in the north of England as he couldn't bear the Scottish weather, which is relentlessly dismal (not that England is exactly Hawaii).

As for Balliol, he embraced the chance to retire in England where he'd 'dwell there in the ways that used to be his, and would hunt in his parks, and do what he wished for his solace and pleasure.' However, before he quit, Edward decided to humiliate him with an act of ceremonial 'degradation' at Montrose in which the Lion of Scotland was ripped from his surcoat, or tabard, earning him the nickname Toom (empty) Tabard.

Edward wanted to build lots of castles in Scotland as he had in Wales, but they had run out of money and could only afford wood by that point. In fact, between 1294 and 1304, the king spent a million pounds on war, a vast fortune at the time that led to widespread discontent (as a rough estimate, one pound then corresponds to $1,000 in today's money, although changes in the cost of living make such conversions inexact). In 1297, there was open revolt by the aristocracy and so, in response, Edward reissued what turned out to be the final, definite Magna Carta, establishing certain fundamental freedoms under English law such as the right to not be arrested without charge.

However, in order to raise money for a Crusade in the Holy Land—still his lifelong goal—Edward sent agents to raid people's savings, including eleven thousand pounds taken from private deposits. They forced their way into ecclesiastical buildings with axes and smashed up chests. When the elderly Dean of St. Paul went to deliver the clergy's response, he collapsed and died in terror at having to confront the king. Not one to tread on people's sensibilities, Edward still sent knights to the dead man's colleagues saying he would have their money or they would be in trouble. He ended up outlawing the clergy en masse after they refused to hand over cash, with royal agents taking their food and livestock. When Roger Bigod in Parliament in 1297 questioned why he should have to help fight Edward's wars, the king replied 'Either you will go or you will hang' to a stunned assembly.

King Edward also tried to recover crown lands that had been lost during the reign of his father with a new scheme called *Quo Warranto*, 'by what right,' whereby royal officials would turn up at people's homes and demand to know by what right they owned the land. The Earl of Gloucester,[6] when asked this question, famously showed them his big sword and shouted 'Behold, my lords. This warrant. For my ancestors came with William the Bastard and conquered their lands with the swords—and by the sword I shall defend them from anyone wishing to seize them.' Which they took as a reasonable answer.

In 1299, a truce between England and France was agreed upon, by which the king would marry Princess Margaret and his son Edward would marry her sister Isabella, all of which seems a bit weird. However, there soon emerged yet another Scottish uprising, and another mass of mad-looking people crossed the border and terrorized the north of England. As Walter of Guisborough put it: 'In all the monasteries and churches between Newcastle and Carlisle the service of God totally ceased, for all the canons, monks, and priests fled before the Scots, as did nearly all the people.'

Edward called his barons to join him in another assault, but many refused because he had milked them for so much money, and so his invasion force of Scotland in 1298 was mostly Welsh, Irish, and Gascon. It was hard to get English knights to go to Scotland because there was almost nothing to steal; Edward I even offered to pay knights for military service in 1282, but they refused, perhaps seeing it as an insult.

A new figure emerged at this point. In 1296, there had been a court reference to one 'William le Waleys, a thief,' but the great Scottish leader is first mentioned by English chroniclers the following year when they describe him as 'a chief of brigands' and 'a vagrant and a fugitive.'

William Wallace, as fans of *Braveheart* will know, became involved because the local English sheriff killed his wife, although what the film didn't mention is that this was in revenge for Wallace murdering the sheriff's son because he had offended Wallace by making a disparaging comment about his clothes. According to another story, Wallace also got into a fatal fight when an English soldier said: 'What's a Scot need a knife like that, as the monk said who last screwed your wife?' Wallace also had an English treasurer called Cressingham skinned and turned into a belt, on top of many other atrocities, so he was not quite the romantic figure many would like to believe. Wallace 'adhered to no rules of chivalry, but waged total war against man, woman, and child,' as one chronicler put it.

Being from a gentry family, Wallace wouldn't have painted himself blue in the ancient Pictish style any more than the commander-in-chief of Her Majesty's Armed Forces would walk around today dressed as a Tudor minstrel.[7] Much of the Wallace story, including an early form of the subplot where Longshanks's second wife falls for Wallace, comes from a poet called 'Blind Harry' who lived two hundreds year later, hardly the kind of testimony that would stand up in court.

The invasion was a disaster to start with. Drunken fighting between English and Welsh infantrymen led the latter to withdraw and then threaten to side with the Scots. Edward replied, sounding rather like Grand Moff Tarkin ordering the destruction of a planet in *Star Wars*: 'Who cares if our enemies joined together? We shall beat them both in a day.'

With Wallace leading the rebellion, other noblemen now joined in, including the powerful barons, James Stewart and William

Douglas. (Douglas had married his wife by simply kidnapping her, one of the exciting ancient Scandinavian traditions that hadn't entirely died out in the area.)

In September 1297, the Scots won a rare victory at Stirling Bridge, which was only wide enough for men in two-by-two formation. However, after some initial heroism and glory, the Scots always lose these wars, and the following year at Falkirk, the inevitable happened. The Scots were on the side of a hill in a hedgehog formation and realizing they could not win, their nobles fled the field. For the battle, Edward had large new windows put in the queen's chambers nearby so 'she and her ladies could observe their gallant menfolk in action,' this being medieval men's idea of what women found attractive.[8]

The English were helped in this conflict by enormous siege machines that had to be dragged by several thousand men and that could lob huge amounts of artillery at the enemy. One of these trebuchets, 'the War Wolf,' especially excited King Edward, and he even refused a surrender because he wanted to try out his new toy. (Trebuchets often had scary names, such as 'God's Stone Thrower' or 'the Furious.') The Scots, meanwhile, had to rely on more low-tech but equally gruesome tricks, one of which was to trap English soldiers on a bridge, knock the bridge down, and leave the soldiers to drown in their armor.

Even the King of England was almost killed at one point when a crossbow bolt went through his clothes while he was riding around the walls; on another occasion, stones from a catapult scared his horse, which threw him.

While a war of independence was going on, many Scots were also engaged in ongoing feuds with other Scots, and Wallace was eventually captured by a Scottish nobleman and was handed over to the English in 1305, then taken to London where he was tried for treason. Obviously, he wasn't going to be found Not Guilty and was soon hanged, drawn, and quartered near what is now the city's fashionable Smithfield Market, having first been dragged naked through the streets. He was also castrated before having his stomach cut open and his bowels burned before him.

Wallace's body was taken to the four corners not just of England but of Britain, and his head was stuck on a pike in London. The Great Seal of Scotland, the symbol of authority and law in that country, was then presented to the king who threw it to one side, musing philosophically, 'A man does good business when he rids himself of a turd.'

But while Wallace was dead, he had the last laugh; soon after the release of Mel Gibson's film in 1995, John Major's despised government sent the Stone of Scone back up to Scotland in a desperate attempt to make the Conservative Party less hated there (it didn't work—the following year they lost all their seats at the General Election).

But now came the moment for another Scottish hero, Robert the Bruce. Bruce was no angel either, and the Church refused to support his Scottish independence struggle because he'd murdered a rival in church. This occurred in February 1306, before the high altar of the Franciscan church at Dumfries where Bruce stabbed to death John Comyn of Badenoch, former guardian of Scotland, and had himself declared king. In response, Robert's sister Mary Bruce and another woman, the Countess of Buchan, who had crowned Robert, were taken prisoner and stuck in wooden cages by Edward. They were lucky; any man who supported Robert was executed, including three brothers and three brothers-in-law.

Longshanks also began to execute Scottish noblemen. John of Athollwas the first earl put to death by an English king since 1076, something considered against the rules of chivalry. He did at least give Atholl a special exemption in that he was hanged on gallows thirty feet higher than his fellow, common prisoners, after which he was beheaded and burned. (It's important in Britain to have these class distinctions, even during executions.) He then had Bruce's sister-in-law Isabella, Countess of Buchan, stuck in a cage for participating at his coronation. Edward had begun a spiral of brutalization in Britain that reached its nadir the following century with the War of the Roses, but it was partly because he was more concerned with the idea of law. He saw people rebelling against him not as rival warlords, as his ancestors might have done, but as traitors.

On the run from his enemies, both English and Scottish, Robert the Bruce now realized his only hope was to present himself as an anti-English independence leader. At one point, in perhaps the most famous incident of the Wars of Independence, Bruce was hiding in a cave and, while there, watched a spider attempt to attach a thread to a beam, failing to do so six times. The spider stuck at it and achieved it the seventh time around, and this inspired Bruce to persevere.[9]

And so with a fresh Scottish revolt in 1306, Edward, now sixty-eight, marched north once again, vowing he would not sleep two nights in the same place until the rebels were defeated. Before setting off, he held a Whit Sunday banquet at Westminster Abbey, known since as The Feast of Swans. Here he bestowed knighthood on his son Edward and three hundred other young men; the king swore two oaths, one to avenge himself of Robert the Bruce and the other to go on Crusade—which at his age must have looked pretty unlikely. The king's son then swore he would not sleep two nights in the same place until he had followed his father's mission to crush the Scots, and all the other young knights swore to follow him. The younger Edward, who preferred basket weaving to fighting, clearly had no intention of doing this, and such oaths were often made at feasts where people had drunk a lot. Various chronicles from the Crusades record men swearing to go to Jerusalem while hopelessly drunk then waking up terrified.

After this lavish ceremony, a grand tournament was held to celebrate the future king and his glorious rule (with two fatalities, which wasn't especially bad for sporting events in the period).

However, near the border, Longshanks came down with dysentery and died; according to popular legend, even with his dying breath the king demanded that servants carry his bones around Scotland, having boiled them down, until the rebels were crushed. Sadly this probably isn't true.

Edward's death was kept a secret for a fortnight and anyone who talked about it was imprisoned, but when the public learned of it there was great sorrow; as was always the case in medieval Europe, people liked to be ruled by a strong man, even a cruel and oppressive one who treated them terribly. One writer lamented that Edward had outshined 'not only Arthur and Alexander but also Brutus, Solomon, and Richard the Lionheart,' adding, 'We should perceive him to surpass all the kings of the earth who came before him.' A Westminster obituary writer said Edward was peaceable to the obedient 'but to the sons of pride he was indeed "a terrible king."' His gravestone in Westminster reads: 'Edward the First, Hammer of the Scots. Keep Faith.' There was no effigy, perhaps on his son's orders; the two did not like each other.

There were some good aspects to the king. He was very well traveled for the time, having gone all over Western Europe, North Africa, and Cyprus, although to be fair these were almost entirely for battles. Edward also commissioned surveys of England that led to the first maps being made of the country, and before then there was almost no geographical knowledge in Western Europe; however, his motivation was probably less wonderment at the world and more a desire to invade the places on the map.

The same could be said for the other main development of his reign: Parliament. Because his wars were so relentlessly expensive, he was forced to give more and more say to the Lords and Commons. The Gascony crisis of 1294–1303, in the words of one historian, led to the 'creation of state finances by parliamentary taxation.'[10] In essence, he created Parliament as we know it, even if this wasn't necessarily his intention.

CHAPTER FOUR

Famine

An Unconventional King

Had it not been for the relentless tragedy of fourteenth-century life, Edward I would have been followed by Alfonso I. But his eldest son passed away before him, joining a list of unlikely sounding English kings who died before their time, among them Eustace, Arthur, Frederick, and Ralph (nephew of Edward the Confessor who, had he not died in 1057, may well have inherited the throne a decade later).

Instead, the crown passed to his only surviving son, Edward, who, though tall, blond, and athletic, would be a grave disappointment to his father. Edward II spent most of his time with handsome court 'favorites,' a medieval version of the gossip column's 'pop star and close friend,' and preferred basket weaving, thatching, gardening, and other early forms of DIY to soldiering, which in the rather unenlightened minds of the average medieval person were seen as unworthy of a king. But the most undignified of his pursuits was rowing, since no king should ever need to pick up an oar, in the same way as a gangster might lose respect if he turned up to a crime family meeting on a bicycle wearing a helmet.

Edward II was also into amateur dramatics and a 'minstrel fanatic,' which might have had something to do with the fact that he was raised by a nurse who was also a part-time minstrel; at his coronation, he paid for 154 musicians to play. On one occasion, the king gave 'Jack of St. Albans' fifty shillings because 'he danced before the king on a table and made him laugh very greatly.' Edward also paid a cook twenty shillings 'because he rode before the King . . . and often fell from his horse,' which also made the king laugh 'very greatly'—snippets that suggest he wasn't a great intellectual titan. He also lost a lot of money in betting and playing pitch-and-toss.

People often complained that King Edward's countenance was unregal, that he preferred gardening to soldiering and liked to mingle with 'harlots and jesters.' He also enjoyed the company of 'mechanicals' and 'buffoons, singers, actors, carters, ditchers, oarsmen, and sailors,' according to a contemporary chronicler, Ranulf Higden.

Most controversially of all, he liked to swim, which was considered not just unmanly, but actually sinister to the medieval mind, 'the spooky embrace of an unnatural element.'[1] Even sailors and fishermen considered it bad luck to learn to swim and, unsurprisingly, a lot of them drowned. In February 1303, it was recorded that the king had gone swimming with 'Robert the Fool,' mixing his two favorite pastimes. He wasn't totally uncultured, however, and he was the first English monarch to found a college: King's Hall, Cambridge.

Edward II's reign would begin disastrously, and would only get worse. According to one historian, he was 'arguably the worst and ultimately the most dangerous king ever to rule England.'[2] Another described him as 'one of the best examples of the brutal and brainless athletes who ended up on the throne.'[3]

Edward was cursed with having poor judgment in people, most likely a result of his lonely, sad childhood. He was the youngest of sixteen, and almost all of his siblings were either far older or deader than him; his mother passed away when he was only six and his father was away for most of his childhood starting wars, hardly the best environment to raise a child. Longshanks was certainly not from the hugs-and-kisses school of parenting, being prone to boxing children on the ear when they annoyed him; as well as throwing his daughter's crown in a fire, he once ripped Edward II's hair out in a rage. The cause was Piers Gaveston.

Gaveston was a minor nobleman from Gascony, and had been Edward's friend from a young age; their relationship was intimate and most likely sexual. It was Longshanks who had selected Gaveston as a companion for his son, and when the king took them campaigning in Scotland they hung around each other all the time, so much so that the court chroniclers compared them to David and Jonathan, 'the great biblical example of friendship between two men,' although the Old Testament prophets probably wouldn't have entirely approved of their relationship.

However, it was noted by a London chronicler that a year before his death, the old king 'saw that his son, the Prince of Wales, had an inordinate love for a certain Gascon knight,' and lost his temper a bit. When Edward II asked his father to give the county of Ponthieu in northern France to Gaveston, which young Edward owned through his mother, he replied: 'You bastard son of a bitch! Now you want to give lands away—you who never gained any? As the Lord lives, were it not for fear of breaking up the kingdom, you should never enjoy your inheritance.'

Late in 1306, Gaveston had deserted the king's campaign in Scotland along with twenty-one other young knights to go to a tournament. He was pardoned in January 1307, but then a month later was banished from England and banned from returning without permission from the king. Before he left, young Edward gave Piers two tourneying outfits in green emblazed with Gaveston's coat of arms; one in fine linen, the other in velvet embroidered with pearls and piping of silver and gold. Not something that male friends normally do for each other.

So when the old king died, Edward immediately recalled his favorite and had him made Earl of Cornwall before his father was even buried. Five days after the funeral, he had Piers married to his niece Margaret, with the new monarch guest of honor at Berkhamsted Castle for the marriage ceremony. He even paid for the bride and groom to be showered with silver pennies.

Edward kept a chamber for Gaveston close to his own, and six months into his reign made him 'keeper of the realm.' The two men even wore the same clothes when they were holding court. Their relationship soon caused tremendous resentment among the nobility, not necessarily because it was sexual, but because of the favoritism and the perks his 'minion' was getting, perks historically owned by the leading noble families. Gaveston also seemed to have that great gift of annoying everyone and, to make matter worse, he was also a foreigner and fairly lowborn, being from a minor noble family.

But no one was angrier at the relationship than Edward's new wife Isabella, the strong-willed and highly intelligent twelve-year-old daughter of Philippe of France. Just a month after Edward and Isabella's marriage came the disastrous coronation, wherein Edward displayed a coat of arms representing himself and Gaveston, and sat with the man instead of his new wife throughout the celebration. By the end of 1308, the leading lords were demanding Edward get rid of the Gascon. Gaveston's arrogance was 'intolerable to the barons, and a prime cause of hatred and rancour'; he made enemies by giving powerful barons bitchy nicknames, such as 'whoreson' for the Earl of Gloucester, 'the fiddler' for the Earl of Leicester, and 'the black hound' for Warwick. 'Let him call me hound,' Warwick told his allies, 'one day the hound will bite him.'

The barons were further infuriated because Gaveston was also a brilliant fighter, holding tournaments where he beat everyone in sight. Later that year, a number of noblemen asked the king to remove Gaveston, so Edward made him Regent of Ireland, where he did a terrible job, but he soon returned uninvited. With the war in Scotland being lost, a group of barons—led by the king's fantastically rich cousin Thomas, Earl of Lancaster, a man with a private army larger than the king's—set up a committee called the Lords Ordainers, and demanded reform of the Crown.

In February 1310, a group of lords arrived at Parliament armed and angry. The king was forced to give into their demand that he appoint a body of twenty-one Ordainers, lords who would 'ordain and establish the estate of our household and of our realm.' The rebels stated that 'unless the king granted their demands, they would not have him for king, nor keep the fealty that they had sworn to him.'

To distract from all his problems, Edward decided to invade Scotland and take Gaveston with him, forcing Queen Isabella, still only fifteen, to come along. It didn't go well. Most of the earls wouldn't join them, while Robert the Bruce wouldn't play by the established rules of war by meeting the English on open ground, but instead conducted guerrilla fighting. In the end, Edward spent eight futile months at Berwick getting nowhere, and so he and Isabella rode south in July 1311.

While Gaveston stayed as the king's lieutenant in Scotland, Edward returned to be confronted by forty-one fresh demands from the Lords Ordainers. Some of these reflected the growing importance of Parliament and its evolution into a check on royal power: they demanded that the lords in Parliament were to be king's advisers with the power to vet all royal appointments; that the king could only wage war with baronial consent; that Parliament must have more say in financial matters; and that all revenue must be paid into the treasury all important and serious issues that have some bearing on politics today. Their main concern, however, was that he get rid of Gaveston.

Edward protested that they 'stop persecuting my brother Piers,' but he eventually agreed and the Earl of Cornwall was exiled in November 1311, for the third time. However, at Christmas, in a soap-opera like scene, Gaveston turned up in England yet again, and the following month he was with the king in York. The rebellion stepped up now.

In February 1311, the leading critical baron, Henry Lacy, Earl of Lincoln, had died; he had been a force for moderation, and with him gone, leadership of the opposition passed to his son-in-law, Thomas of Lancaster. Lancaster was the son of Edward I's brother Edmund, held huge amounts of land in the North, had an enormous private army, and was 'acutely conscious of his own preeminent position among the English nobility, set apart as he was from his peers both by birth and by the scale of his wealth and power.'[4] As well as being the cousin of Edward II, he was also the uncle of Isabella, his mother having been the granddaughter of Louis VIII. He already owned large areas of Lancashire, Leicester, and Derby, and his marriage to the heiress Alice Lacy meant he also got Lincoln and Salisbury, too. He was 'a loner, aloof and haughty,' and did not get on with the other opponents of the king, their only bond being a shared hatred of Gaveston.

By this stage, the queen hated Gaveston so much that her father Philippe IV paid two earls to plot against him after Isabella complained of his behavior, but he withdrew after she was given the county of Ponthieu by her husband.

While Edward and his lover were on the border, the rebel lords marched north to confront them, improbably claiming they were only heading up to a tournament, and just happened to have a really large army with them. At the end of April, Lancaster arrived at Newcastle and Edward fled by sea with Gaveston, leaving weapons, jewels, and horses behind, as well as his now-pregnant wife. This was the first of two occasions in which he'd deserted Isabella, but in fairness to Edward the sea journey would have been too dangerous for her unborn child. She also had nothing to fear if captured, unlike Gaveston; as it was, the two men spent a miserable five-day voyage in rough seas, which must have been especially grim for Piers as he had recently been ill.

Edward was hopeless as king, but no historian has anything nice to say about the 'mediocrities' opposed to him:[5] Lancaster was 'sulky, vindictive, self-seeking, brutal, and vicious,' the Earl of Warwick was 'treacherous,' and another malcontent, Seward de Warenne, the Earl of Surrey, was 'a disreputable nonentity.' Warwick in particular had that very Renaissance combination of being both very interested in high culture and literature, and also a cruel sadist.[6]

Gaveston would soon experience this firsthand. He was besieged in Scarborough and surrendered to the Earl of Pembroke, a critical but loyal supporter of the crown who swore to take care of his prisoner. However, when Pembroke went away to see his wife Beatrice, Warwick, knowing that Gaveston was unguarded, assembled an army and rode the twenty-five miles to Pembroke's Castle, in Deddington. Pembroke's soldiers laid down their arms and Warwick shouted from outside his windows: 'Get up traitor—you are taken.'[7] The poor man was 'led forth not as an earl but as a thief' and, on June 19, was handed over to Lancaster's men and dragged two miles to Blacklow Hill, first on foot at the end of a rope and then by an old horse. Finally, on Lancaster's orders, a soldier stabbed Gaveston and, as he fell, another took a sword out and chopped off his head. The Earl of Cornwall's body was left to rot in a field and was eventually rescued by monks.

According to a chronicler, the killers 'knew that when the matter came to the king's notice, he would, if he could, proceed to take vengeance.'[8] Naturally, Edward was devastated, and on the anniversary of his lover's death he traveled to France to be entertained by 'Bernard the Fool and fifty-four naked dancers.' We all get through these things in our own way.

A few months later, the queen gave birth to a son, which her family insisted on calling Louis, but which the English lords vetoed in favor of Edward; Londoners who just weeks earlier feared their city would be caught up in a civil war partied in the streets with free wine, which was always given out during such events, and which inevitably led to multiple casualties.

The royal couple soon headed for France, where things might have appeared all in order to observers; Edward and Isabella over-slept for one event and the French hosts indulgently let them be, assuming it was down to Edward wanting to stay in bed with a beautiful wife, probably making ze sweet love. Which was probably unlikely.[9] In July, the lords had assembled in London and had to wait while the king didn't appear or even send word.

Bannockburn

To turn attention away from his incompetence, Edward invaded Scotland in 1314, managing to suffer one of the most humiliating defeats in English history. The battle of Bannockburn, in which Robert the Bruce's men were outnumbered two-to-one by the English, was fought in 'an evil, deep, and wet marsh' and, while the terrain didn't help, Edward's disastrous leadership was mostly to blame. Two leading noblemen, the Earls of Hereford and Gloucester, had bickered over who would lead, and the king dithered, offering them joint command. Eventually, Gloucester was so full of rage he decided to win the argument by single-handedly charging at the Scots. He was hacked to death instantly, which at least resolved the question of who was in charge.

In the ensuing battle, some one thousand Englishmen were killed, among them twenty-two barons and sixty-eight knights, and more lost their lives in the fifty-mile pursuit that followed. To cap the disaster, the Privy Seal, the highly symbolic personal insignia of the monarch, was also taken. The Scots lost just two knights and five hundred pike men, having used low-tech skills to beat a more advanced enemy, digging and then covering up holes around the English lines, into which many fell.

Edward fled back south, lucky to escape with his life, after which years of raids continued in northern England, and at one point one-fifth of the country was paying tribute to the Scottish king.

Meanwhile Robert's brother, Edward Bruce, invaded Ireland and declared himself king there.

Then the crops failed. Europe was becoming much colder after four warm centuries, during which London enjoyed the same climate as central France today; wine production in England ended in 1250 and would not return for centuries, while cereal growing retreated in Scandinavia and the European colony in Greenland was abandoned to its fate.[10]

The changing weather was the major factor in a wider economic depression linked to wars in Asia Minor in the 1250s and in France in the 1290s. Back in 1289, a great storm ruined the harvest, and, in 1309–1310, the Thames froze, while the Baltic turned to ice twice that decade. There had been five famines in England between 1272 and 1311, but 'between 1315 and 1319 came a crescendo of calamity.'[11]

Johannes de Trokelowe, a Benedictine monk at the time, wrote: 'In the year of our Lord 1315, apart from the other hardships with which England was afflicted, hunger grew in the land . . . Meat and eggs began to run out, capons and fowl could hardly be found, animals died of pest, swine could not be fed because of the excessive price of fodder . . . The land was so oppressed with want that when the king came to St. Albans on the feast of St. Laurence [10 August] it was hardly possible to find bread on sale to supply his immediate household.'

The lack of sun also hindered the production of salt, which made meat preservation harder, while many animals drowned in the floods, which also increased the number of parasites and crop diseases. There was misery 'such as our age has never seen,' and people were reduced to digging up the newly buried to eat, while in Poland it was reported that starving peasants had been taking down hanged men from gibbets. According to one chronicler, the poor ate 'dogs, cats, the dung of doves, even their own children.'

At least the Great Famine also killed any hopes of a great Celtic alliance against England. The Scots had invaded Ireland to 'liberate' it, and though there may have been some good intentions somewhere, these disappeared as their soldiers became so hungry that they even dug up fresh graves. Native churchmen complained that the Scots were even worse than the English, and they 'left neither wood nor lea, nor corn nor crop nor stead nor barn nor church, but fired and burnt them all.' Ireland's Anglo-Norman elite had more in common with the native Irish than the French-speaking Bruces; many Anglo-Irish had become 'degenerates,' as the English described it, adopting the Irish language, law, and custom.[12]

There was also a huge increase in crime back in England, which was already absurdly violent by today's standards. In fact, government attempts to fight crime were often resented by civic leaders, many of whom were at least responsible for some of the violence, so that when Edward I introduced a crackdown in 1304, 'a contemporary songsmith who purported to be a war veteran complained that, as a result of the new measures, good men like himself were being falsely accused and unjustly imprisoned, simply because they had knocked their servants about a bit.'[13]

Edward II's reign was so violent the country was terrorized by heavily armed middle-class gangs known as 'trail bastons,' the worst being the Folvilles, a Leicestershire gentry family who for a decade committed numerous murders, rapes, and robberies near to their home of Ashby Folville, called the 'Castle of the Four Winders.' In 1326, they killed a senior tax collector and, in 1332, kidnapped and ransomed a royal judge, Sir Richard Willoughby. Along with another criminal gang, the Coterel brothers, they made life a misery for people in large areas of Nottinghamshire and Derbyshire.

However, the judge in question was largely hated and the gang was popular with the sort of people who always idolize violent outlaws; 'Folville's Law' became used as a term to mean robbery of someone who probably deserved it. As the old joke goes, they were halfway to becoming Robin Hood—stealing from the rich, without getting around to giving it to the poor.

Many criminals came to horrific ends: Richard Folville, a vicar of all things, was eventually dragged away from church by armed men and beheaded. However, many outlaws eventually received pardons after fighting in the English army in Scotland or France, among them at least two of Friar Richard's brothers, as well as notorious outlaws such as Sir William de Chetulton and Sir John de Legh, and another gang leader, James Stafford.

This was a period where violence was far more common than today, and from unlikely sources. Among the most notorious priest gangs were the clergy from Lichfield Cathedral who helped the Coterel brothers on occasion, while on October 18, 1327, the monks of Bury St. Edmunds went to the nearby parish church where they burst in with armor and seized several citizens. When townsfolk went to the abbey to demand their release, the monks replied with missiles, killing many people. A large army was summoned, which included twenty-eight chaplains, and the abbey was set alight and stormed.

Historian Barbara Hanawalt recalled one incident in Northamptonshire when 'a certain William of Wellington, parish chaplain of *Yelvertoft*, sent John, his clerk, to John Cobbler's house to buy a candle for him for a penny. But John would not send it to him without the money wherefore William became enraged, and, knocking in the door upon him, he struck John in the front part of the head so that his brains flowed forth and he died forthwith.'

The homicide rate in England was at least ten times what it is today, with London having a higher murder level than the most dangerous American cities in the early twenty-first century; the vast majority of murderers escaped justice, although if they were caught the punishment was gruesome. While today the poor are far more likely to be the victims and perpetrators of violence, the opposite was true in the fourteenth and fifteenth centuries, when some 26 percent of male English aristocrats died from violence, compared to roughly 0.4 percent of American men today.[14]

Almost every area of life was more violent. Popular sports at the time consisted of events in which 'players with hands tied behind them competed to kill a cat nailed to a post by battering it to the death with their heads, at the risk of cheeks ripped open or eyes scratched out by the frantic animal's claws'; alternatively men would beat to death a pig in a pen with clubs 'to the laughter of spectators.'[15] Everyone considered this great fun, accompanied by the sound of trumpeters playing in the background.

The most popular form of entertainment at the time were religious 'mystery' plays, which featured scenes from the Bible played out by actors, but were far more like an HBO series than Golden Age Hollywood. When John the Baptist was decapitated, 'the actor was whisked away so cunningly in exchange for a fake corpse and fake head spilling ox blood that the audience shrieked in excitement.'[16] A man playing Jesus would be tied to the cross for three hours reciting verse, often in agony.

Religious plays were put together by the various guilds of each city, comprising the different trades, and often ended in mass brawls between actors. At Chester in 1399, there was a running battle between weavers and fullers during the procession; twenty years later at York, carpenters and shoemakers attacked skinners, using clubs and axes. At Newcastle, laws were introduced against 'the dissension and discord that hath been amongst the Crafts of the said Towne as of man slaughter and murder and other mischiefs.'

This violence went right to the top, and increased after the death of Gaveston, when Edward's behavior became increasingly bizarre. In 1317, he came under the spell of Nicholas of Wisbech, a fraudulent friar who claimed to own a vial of holy oil given to Thomas Becket; the king believed that if he were re-anointed with this oil, all the political troubles in England would end and he would also be able to conquer the Holy Land. The pope said no.

In 1318, a lunatic cleric called John Powderham turned up at Beaumont Palace in Oxford claiming to be the rightful son of Edward I. He argued that the so-called monarch was in reality a carter's son and they had been mixed up as babies. He was clearly mad, and the king thought of keeping him as a fool. Today, Powderham would probably have a popular blog revealing the 'real truth' the mainstream media would be too biased to reveal. However, people were unhappy enough with the monarch to entertain the idea that maybe Powderham was onto something, so the king had him hanged. During his trial, the poor man claimed that his pet cat was possessed and had incited him, so the cat was hanged, too. The execution of this madman infuriated the queen 'beyond words'; there were already signs of a deep problem with their marriage. (Isabella had a charitable side, once ensuring that a Scottish orphan boy she met on the road was given new clothes and sent to London to be taught and given medical help for the disease of the scalp from which he was suffering.)

In the meantime, the opposition was weakened by various mutual hatreds. The Earl of Surrey had been in a loveless and childless marriage to Jeanne of Bar, the king's niece, and for a number of years had wanted to marry his mistress, with whom he already had two sons. He and Lancaster did not get on, and so Lancaster supported the Church's refusal to grant an annulment. In retaliation, Surrey abducted Lancaster's wife, Alice Lacy. They also had an unhappy marriage, so she may have colluded in the stunt, and this public humiliation led to a private war between the two men.

The only thing that united them was a hatred of the court favorite, and luckily, after the fall of Gaveston, Edward adopted a new, even worse one, Hugh Despenser the Younger, along with his father Hugh Despenser the Elder. Despenser the Younger was 'a menacing predator, as opposed to Gaveston's distracting peacock,'[17] and was notorious for having murdered a captive, Llewelyn Bren, in horrific fashion, after he had surrendered. Despenser was greedy and ruthless, and, having married the king's niece Eleanor, was intent on increasing his power base in the West; he tried to grab land owned by a Marcher family on the Welsh border, the once mighty de Briouzes, and also alienated Roger Mortimer, the leading magnate in the region. While the country was suffering famine, the younger Despenser was putting vast amounts of gold into banks in Florence. The queen disliked the Despensers intensely, and on her knees she begged her husband to get rid of them, but to no avail.

In the spring of 1321, Marcher lords led by Roger Mortimer mobilized for a meeting in Yorkshire with Lancaster and other northern barons. Parliament was surrounded by the armed retainers of the barons, and the Despensers were banished. The younger Despenser became a pirate.

Lancaster tried to go into alliance with Robert the Bruce, but Bruce didn't trust him, partly because Lancaster kept referring to himself as 'King Arthur' during negotiations, which made the Scotsman suspect he wasn't entirely well.

Briefly, Edward's luck changed and he seemed to turn everything around. He defeated a rebellion by Mortimer, with the help of the Welsh, and Despenser, now back on land, captured Thomas of Lancaster in Yorkshire. The king's cousin was put on trial in a kangaroo court and was soon found guilty. Edward agreed he should be spared hanging in tribute to his royal blood so, at Pontefract in Yorkshire in March 1322, his head was cut off. Dressed in rags and wearing a ripped hat, Lancaster was bundled onto an old mare and forced to ride to his execution in sleet while locals pelted him with snowballs before being forced to kneel, facing Scotland, which he was accused of conspiring with. He was killed with 'two or three clumsy strokes' until eventually his head came off, the first member of the royal family to be executed since the Norman conquest.

This was followed a week later by the murder of six leading Lancastrians, among them John Mowbray who was hanged at York on March 2, and another rebel, Bartholomew Badlesmere, who was dragged through Canterbury by horses and taken to a crossroads where he was hanged and decapitated.

Dozens were sent to prison, among them Alice Lay, Lancaster's widow, who was told she would be burned to death unless she gave most of her possessions to Despenser and his father. Mortimer was condemned to be executed, but this was commuted to being locked up in the Tower, in quarters that were 'less elegant than they were seemly.'

The 'judicial murder' of Lancaster shocked the country and a cult soon grew around his tomb in Pontefract Priory, where it was said that a drowned child returned to life and a blind priest had his sight restored. To mock this, a servant of Hugh Despenser defecated on the same spot, but it was said—the medieval chronicler version of 'some guy told me'—that later his bowels were parted from his body. A stone table in St. Paul's commemorating Lancaster became the setting for further supposed miracles, surrounded by weeping, hysterical imbeciles.

In August 1322, Edward invaded Scotland and declared that 'we have found no resistance,' but this was only because the Scots had simply disappeared beyond the River Forth to conduct the usual guerrilla warfare. The English troops retreated with their loot, which in total added up to one lame cow, but the Scots followed them and, on October 22 at Old Byland in Yorkshire, they inflicted a smaller but more humiliating defeat than Bannockburn. The English soldiers ran away and Edward fled to the coast where a boat took him to safety, leaving his jewels and the captured Earl of Richmond.

For a second time, he had left his wife at the mercy of his enemies, for Isabella—in Tynemouth Priory in Northumberland—was cut off by the Scots. Edward sent her letters but made no attempt at rescue, and instead ordered for Despenser's cronies to come. She refused to go, as she didn't trust them, and finally escaped by sea, where two of her ladies died en route, one in labor and another falling overboard.

Edward ruled in a way that didn't exactly command loyalty. In 1323, Andrew Harclay, hero of the battle of Boroughbridge in which Lancaster was defeated, decided that the war could only be ended by negotiating with Robert the Bruce. So he met him. However, when Edward and Despenser learned of this, they had him immediately executed, and it was decreed that Harclay should be drawn, hanged, and beheaded: 'That your heart, and bowels and entrails, whence came your traitorous thoughts, be torn out and burnt to ashes and that the ashes be scattered to winds; that your body be cut into four quarters,' and sent to Carlisle, Newcastle, York, and Shrewsbury, and the head set on London Bridge.

Then, in 1324, the new king of France, Isabella's brother Charles IV, invaded Gascony; the English defenders had to buy a six-month truce and give away a lot of land. This new Anglo-French war was obviously bad for the queen; Despenser had her lands confiscated and her household was purged, with French subjects interned. On top of this, her three children were taken and put into the custody of Despenser's wife and sister.

Isabella was then sent to France in March 1325 on a diplomatic mission to make peace with her brother, along with a relatively small entourage of thirty-one attendants who had been specially chosen for their loyalty to Despenser. Fatefully, there she would meet Roger Mortimer, who had managed to escape from the Tower on August 1, 1323, using the oldest trick in the book (although maybe it wasn't old at the time). It was the feast day of Saint Peter ad Vincula, patron saint of the Tower church, which was always marked by heavy drinking by the guards. Mortimer's friends had turned Gerard de Alspaye, the sublieutenant of the tower, who spiked everyone's drinks including his own (to make it look like he wasn't involved). They hacked into the side of his cell so Mortimer could crawl into the king's kitchen, and then with a rope ladder he escaped up roofs and walls to the river where a boat took him to Hainault across the North Sea.

After Mortimer escaped, Despenser became convinced that his enemy's supporters were using necromancy—black magic—and he wrote to the pope complaining he was threatened by their 'magical and secret dealings.' The pope was not persuaded and replied that no remedies were necessary, only that 'the Holy Father recommends him to turn to God with his whole heart.' Which wasn't likely.

In France, Isabella met her brother Charles who agreed to confirm English possession of Gascony without forcing King Edward to come to Paris to do homage, but instead allowing his eldest son Edward to do so instead. The queen persuaded the king to allow Prince Edward to travel to France to spare him the humiliation of doing so, after which they would both return. He agreed, a fatal error, and after the boy followed his mother in September 1325, the Despensers soon realized they had been outwitted. With the prince in her possession, Isabella was far more dangerous.

King Edward ordered his son and wife to return; otherwise, she would 'feel his wrath all the days of his life.' She said no, Charles refused to expel his sister, and Prince Edward preferred to stay with his mother.

Isabella had complained: 'I feel that marriage is a joining together of man and woman, and someone has come between my husband and myself trying to break this bond. I protest that I will not return until this intruder is removed, but, discarding my marriage garment, [I] shall assume the robes of widowhood and mourning until I am avenged of this Pharisee.' The king, however, seems to have been totally unaware for some time just how much his wife hated him; even in 1321, he ordered special dress-lengths for the queen and her damsel for Christmas, and now that she was in France 'he continued to write to her the puzzled, faintly querulous letters of a kindly husband who cannot imagine what has gone wrong.'[18] What could have upset her?

Roger Mortimer was still in the Flanders at the time and came to France for a funeral where he began a fateful affair with the queen. Roger was a married father of ten, so her family did not entirely approve of the relationship.

Isabella was also joined by King Edward's half brother, the Earl of Kent (who was also Isabella's nephew, confusingly), and leading nobles such as the Earl of Richmond, as well as two senior bishops, who had all turned against the regime. The queen of England was declared an enemy alien and her lands confiscated for the safety of the kingdom, but with a small force she arrived in England in October 1326, along with Mortimer and her son. Edward's other half brother, the Earl of Norfolk, who was in charge of the defense of East Anglia, now went over to Isabella's side.

London's mob showed its support for the invasion the only way it knew how on October 15. That day, Bishop Stapledon, the king's ally, happened to be riding through the city on the way back from a Mass. Walter Stapledon, who was also treasurer, was a man the chronicler *Vita* called 'immeasurably greedy'; he was also one of the first Englishmen to wear glasses, an invention that had just come out of Italy. As agitation against the regime reached fever pitch, the bishop was chased by a mob, and, having tried to get sanctuary at St. Paul's, was dragged off his horse and beheaded with a bread knife. The head was sent to the queen. Meanwhile, Prince Edward was proclaimed 'guardian of the realm' that same month.

Edward and the younger Despenser had tried to flee by boat from Chepstow in Wales, but spent six days at sea, since the wind would not change, and they had to go back, where they were captured. Despenser the Elder had been separated from them days earlier and was caught in Bristol where he was hauled before a tribunal including Mortimer, Lancaster's brother Henry, Kent, and Norfolk. He was obviously not going to be let off, and was dragged through the city streets and hanged from the city gallows. His head was carried on a spear to Winchester; his gruesome punishment seems to have been designed as an ironic parody of Lancaster's. His body was fed to the dogs.

The younger Despenser had tried to starve himself to death while in custody, so they brought the execution forward. Naked but for a crown of nettles and mocking verse carved on his skin with knives, he was dragged through the city of Hereford by four horses to the sound of trumpets and bagpipes, and half hanged on a fifty-foot-tall gallows so that everyone could get a good look. He was stripped and 'hoisted, choking and kicking' by a noose, then the rope was lowered so he could see the executioner's knife coming to castrate him. A fire was lit under the scaffold, and Despenser's genitals were thrown in, followed by his intestines and heart, the dying man watching everything. The crowd cheered as his head was cut off.

In January 1327, Lords and Commons were called in the name of Edward's son, with Mortimer appointed Keeper of the Realm, the first time Parliament effectively chose a king. Mortimer declared that the magnates had deposed Edward because he had not followed his coronation oath and was under the control of evil advisers. The Archbishop of Canterbury concluded that Edward should be deposed because everyone wished it: *vox populi, vox Dei*. In Kenilworth Castle, the king was confronted by his opponents and did not take their advice to abdicate well, 'weeping and fainting.' According to the bishop of Hereford, Edward carried around a knife with which to kill Isabella, and said he'd bite her to death if need be. Clearly the marriage had some problems by this stage.

The king was moved to Berkeley Castle in Gloucestershire, where he was mistreated, mocked, and made to shave off his hair and beard with cold water from a ditch, then dressed in old clothes, with a crown of hay placed on his head, and stuck in a cesspit filled with stinking animal carcasses. It was hoped he'd die of food poisoning, but he proved resilient.

The usurpers moved the king from castle to castle, not knowing what to do with the prisoner, before it was decided that they'd do away with him. Mortimer wanted it to look unsuspicious, so it seems strange that their method of murder was to stick a red-hot poker up his anus. Hardly the most obvious form of suicide anyone would choose.[19]

Although Edward II was a hopeless and tyrannical king, and his wife had every reason to get rid of him, she lost the PR battle. Isabella became known as a *ferrea virago*, a woman who abandoned feminine qualities, or a 'she-wolf,' partly because England would soon become embroiled in a century-long war with her country of birth, but also because she and Mortimer would prove to be just as bad, if not worse, than the regime they replaced.

CHAPTER FIVE

War

The great Italian poet Petrarch wrote toward the end of the century that 'In my youth they [the English] were regarded as the most timid of the uncouth races . . . lower even than the miserable Scots.' In other words, they were barbarians, but not even very effective, scary ones. Compared to Italy, the English certainly were uncouth, but over the next few decades they proved themselves to be anything but timid.

The new king, Edward III, had inherited the strong personalities of his grandfathers, with disastrous consequences for both of their countries. Blessed with the 'face of a god,' according to a contemporary, he was revered by later English rulers as the pinnacle of monarchy and chivalry. The mad King George III, of losing America fame, commissioned Benjamin West to paint scenes of Edward's reign, while Victoria and Albert used to dress up as Edward and his wife Philippa of Hainault. Such was Edward's perceived greatness that even his enemy, France's Charles V, hung a portrait of him in his study.

Edward was the epitome of chivalry and did much to create the pageantry and pomp we associate with England, as well as English national identity, even though it's debatable whether he could even speak English very well and he certainly had to have a tutor.[1] He also brought his country into a brutal, prolonged, and often pointless war, leading thousands of orc-like English criminals across France; funnily enough he was not so appreciated there.

Edward lived for war, was good at it, and clearly enjoyed it. Aged just fifteen, the young king had been put in charge of the English troops on the Scottish border, and at one point he offered to move back a couple of hundred yards from the river so 'that the Scots might have a proper foothold and room to fight.'[2] Things like that gave Edward his reputation for chivalry, although it was also the case that he just loved fighting and would have been disappointed if the Scots had to surrender.

Despite this heroism, Edward comes across as one of the least interesting personalities of the period because he was so lacking in complexity: he loved fighting, women, and sport, and had no major character flaws. He was 'uncomplicated and likeable . . . flamboyant, extrovert, and generous,' loved practical jokes and fancy-dress parties, as well as tournaments, where he fought with the 'same reckless courage that he would later show in battle.'[3] He also had what is now called the common touch, getting on well with the hooligans who constituted most of the English army, playing archery with the foot soldiers, and joking around with his minstrels' kettledrums. Unlike many monarchs of the time, he didn't care about taking revenge and even the sons of enemies could rise up, so that uniquely for this period he had almost 'unconditional political support' among his powerful subjects.[4] But although not begrudging, there was one man he had to remove.

Roger Mortimer had soon made himself hated, and 'lived in a style of pomp and luxury that put the royal court in the shade,' having a Round Table built where jousts and feasts were held.[5] In 1329, he had styled himself as King Arthur at a magnificent tournament with Isabella playing Guinevere; the king's mother, meanwhile, had doubled her already extremely generous annual income. The pair of them quickly wrecked the country's finances, so that crown reserves decreased from over sixty thousand pounds in 1326 to just forty-one pounds in 1330. Mortimer had given himself the grand title Earl of March and became as unpopular as the Despensers, whose lordships he had taken. One historian described him as 'perhaps the nastiest man ever to rule England,' an accolade with some tough competition.[6]

The new regime further lost support by making the realistic but unpopular decision to recognize Scotland's independence. In March 1328, a treaty was signed at Edinburgh in which the English accepted Robert the Bruce as king, with full authority to deal with other heads of state. As part of the deal, Edward's sister Joan was betrothed to Bruce's son David, and young Edward was so angry he didn't attend the marriage ceremony in Berwick, reduced to tears by the 'shameful peace of Northampton.'

Thomas of Lancaster's brother Henry had tried to stay out of politics since inheriting the title, but along with other noblemen he became alarmed at the direction of the government, and, in 1328, he was one of a number to refuse to attend Parliament. In January 1329, Lancaster, along with the king's uncles, the Earls of Kent and Norfolk, marched into London. But Isabella and Mortimer's army attacked their territories in the midlands, and so Lancaster surrendered.

Edmund of Kent was soon arrested on suspicion of treason and then entrapped in a way a Victorian might call 'unsporting.' Mortimer had hired two *agent provocateurs*, Dominican friars, to trick his prisoner into believing his brother Edward II was still alive and was ready to return. There was a rumor that Edward had survived to become a wandering hermit in Cologne, a quite common myth attached to dead medieval kings; Harold II was thought by some to have survived the Battle of Hastings to live as a hermit, while the German Emperor Heinrich V is supposed to have ended up in Cheshire.

Sick of the new regime, Kent fell for the ruse by pledging his support to the former king, and was quickly sentenced to death. On the day of his execution he was led out of Winchester Castle, but he had to wait five hours on the scaffold as no one could be found to behead him until eventually a felon agreed to do the job in exchange for his own death sentence being postponed. When Edmund's head was raised, the crowd remained silent.

The young king, installed as a puppet, could trust so few people that he smuggled a letter to the pope saying only notes with the words *pater sancte*, 'holy father,' could be treated as genuine; otherwise, it could be Mortimer's handiwork. In 1330, he decided to act and, aged just seventeen, led a small band of friends his own age in a *Goonies*-like action-adventure, capturing Mortimer at Nottingham Castle (admittedly an especially violent remake of the *Goonies*). The suspicious Mortimer had every gate and door locked and barred, while the queen looked after the keys and forbade her son from entering, but Edward had told the constable of the castle to leave a door unlocked, and that night he entered the fortress with twenty-five young men. After the teenagers killed three courtiers, Mortimer was captured standing behind a curtain trying to put his armor on.

The queen begged her son to 'spare gentle Mortimer,' but the man responsible for the death of Edward's father was now tried at Westminster while forced to wear a cloak with the phrase *quid gloriaris* emblazed on it—'where's your glory now?' Inevitably, he was sentenced to hang, though spared disembowelment as a concession to Isabella, and his body left to rot for two days at Tyburn. The Tyburn tree, west of London, had been a popular execution spot since 1196 when the populist irritant William Fitzosbert had been hanged, and it remained a place of execution for several centuries, popularly known as 'God's tribunal.' So popular were hangings there that locals would put up temporary stands and charge people to watch, although on one occasion these collapsed, causing dozens of fatalities. The last Tyburn hanging took place in 1763, by which time residents in the increasingly fashionable West End district thought the site of rotting corpses might be lowering the tone of the area a little bit. The spot where the tree stood is now Marble Arch, London's rather feeble imitation of the Arc de Triomphe.[7]

Edward's mother, meanwhile, managed to get off pretty lightly; she was banished to an enormous country estate in Norfolk where her son continued to send her gifts of boar, lovebirds, and wine. She continued to enjoy four thousand pounds a year in allowances and regularly traveled to the capital, where she liked to borrow romance stories from the Tower of London's library. Strangely, at court, Edward would dress as Sir Lancelot and his mother as Lancelot's lover Guinevere, the queen in silk and silver garnished with six hundred rubies and eighteen hundred pearls, and 'attended by minstrels, huntsmen, and grooms.'[8] She died in 1358 and was buried in her wedding gown next to the heart of the husband she utterly despised.

Edward, meanwhile, had enjoyed his first military victory on the boggy ground of Halidon Hill in 1333 against a force of Scots twice as large—the start of a long glorious reign of violence.

116 Years' War

The Victorians called it the Hundred Years' War, although it lasted 116 years and was more like three wars with long intervals in between.[9] The conflict would later become about Edward III's claim to the throne of France through his mother, but it was really about wine, or at least the region where England got its supply: the Duchy of Gascony. The French crown claimed the province, which was still subject to the King of England, and the only way Edward could fight them without losing the support of the pope was to declare himself king of France.

Later, it would turn into a war of naked aggression by the English, without the slightest pretense of any reason except theft. For the ordinary people in regions such as Normandy it was fantastically grim, as their country was overrun by the dregs of England and mercenaries from across Europe, and eventually even Edward lost control of the bands of delinquents running around France. Ultimately, though, the war would not just bankrupt the English crown, but would also lead to what intelligence officials these days call 'blow back'—a civil war back home.

Gascony, the area south of Bordeaux, was ruled by the king of England, although only as a vassal of the king of France, part of the complex system of feudalism that kept the peace but often left some curious anomalies; the French monarch was overlord to most of the regions we now call France even if he sometimes only ruled a small chunk around Paris and much of the rest was in reality independent. Below him were the twelve peers of France—effective rulers in some cases—among them Edward in his role as Duke of Guyenne (another name for Aquitaine, of which Gascony formed the southern part)[10] and Count of Ponthieu.

Bordeaux, a city of thirty thousand people, owed its wealth to wine exports, in particular to the English who drank 'several times more claret per head than they do today.'[11] Wine buffs tend to consider Bordeaux to be the best wine region in the world, and its vintages can sell for vast amounts of money, so it is hardly surprising that the English were keen to keep hold of it. Because of its wine, the region brought in more money for the crown than the whole of England.

The economies of the two countries were closely interlinked, so that the Gascon Henri le Waleys was mayor of both Bordeaux and London. Many Gascons worked in England, often in the army, and took an active part in the wars against the Scots. The Plantagenet monarchs, said one historian, 'regarded Guyenne as a far more integral part of their domains than Wales or Ireland, and Froissart often refers to Guyennois as "the English."'[12] They also regarded the northern French as a separate people, and even as late as the 1789 Revolution referred to those from the North as 'Franchiman' and themselves as 'Romans,' reflecting the fact that northern France had been settled by Germanic Franks while those in the South were more Latin.[13] And with only two hundred English officials in the region, the Gascons were mostly left to run their own affairs, which is why they preferred to be ruled by London rather than Paris.[14]

At the time, France had a population of twenty-one million, compared to just four or five million in England, but France was hopelessly divided and had no real cohesion. Even in the nineteenth century, most people in the country could not speak 'French,' with regional identity being far stronger; England, in contrast, was quite small and homogenous, with the exception of the very far north.

The mirror image of Gascony was Scotland, which the kings of England saw themselves as overlords of, but which the Scots viewed rather differently. Naturally, they formed an 'auld alliance' with France.

The death of Philippe's last son Charles IV in 1328 led to a succession crisis. He left only a pregnant wife and if she produced a son, he would become king; otherwise, the crown would be up in the air with the most likely candidate being a cousin called Philippe of Valois. On April Fool's Day, the widowed queen gave birth to a daughter, so she was forgotten about; Valois got the assembly in Paris to proclaim him Philippe VI.

Both the new kings of France and England were aggressive, alpha-male types—Philippe was a champion jouster—so they were inevitably going to end up fighting, and relations soured fairly quickly. As a prince, Edward had already done homage to the French for Gascony, but, in 1329, Philippe invited him to Amiens to do so again. The Frenchman was furious when his opposite number turned up in a crimson velvet robe with golden leopard prints, sporting a crown on his head along with spurs and a sword. He was supposed to arrive bareheaded, but refused when his overlord demanded it; it was on the basis of such things that wars were started.

The encounter was complicated by numerous conflicts within France, and was stirred up by a succession of embittered aristocrats who arrived at Edward's court encouraging the not-super-bright king to invade. The first of these was Robert of Artois, a leading

French nobleman of dubious virtue, who had fled to England after poisoning his aunt to claim her inheritance for which he was sentenced to death. Robert was described as 'a violent and dishonest adventurer with many enemies' but also 'flamboyant and charming, an excellent horseman and a skillful flatterer, in fact just the kind of man that Edward liked.'[15] Philippe had said anyone who harbored Robert was an enemy, so Edward gave him three castles and made him an earl. In December 1336, the French demanded Robert's extradition, and the following May Philippe VI finally attacked Gascony, so starting the Hundred Years' War effectively.

As Duke of Gascony, Edward could not declare war on his feudal overlord because the pope would excommunicate him. He soon concluded that the only way he could actually take hold of the region was to claim the throne of France itself. By most succession rules Edward had a better case than Philippe, through his mother, but queens could not rule because, as the contemporary historian Froissant said, 'the realm of France was so noble it must not fall into a woman's hands,' and so the French then rationalized that the throne could not even pass through the female line. This Salic Law, supposedly the ancient rule of the Franks, was only made up later. The real reason Edward could not become king was that he was a foreign ruler and Philippe already had a large power base in the country.

It was Robert of Artois who managed to convince Edward to start the war, according to one famous story, by presenting him with a heron at a feast—a deliberate insult since it was considered the coward of the bird world. Edward's response was to swear an oath to 'cross the sea, my subjects with me . . . set the country ablaze and . . . await my mortal enemy, Philippe of Valois, who wears the fleur-delis . . . I renounce him, you can be sure of that, for I will make war on him by word and deed.' This story was satirical, designed to make Edward look idiotic, but he did seem to be easily swayed.

To make matters more complicated, the war also involved Flanders, in what is now Belgium, a very rich country that was theoretically subject to the king of France but was in practice independent with extensive trading links with England. Flanders was divided between its pro-English and pro-French elements, and, in 1338, the pro-English Jacob van Artevelde became 'Hooftman' of Ghent and, after taking most of Flanders, 'put to death anyone who opposed him.' It was his Flemish allies who persuaded Edward to claim the throne because only then could they justify their own behavior by saying they were just doing their duty as vassals of the king of France. Even Edward didn't take the claim seriously, yet he could never drop it without admitting the war was unjust, and so it developed a life of its own. For various reasons, the English didn't officially drop the claim until 1802, by which time there was no king of France anymore, as the last one had his head chopped off in front of a baying mob.

In August 1337, Edward also made a pact with his wife's brother-in-law, the Holy Roman Emperor Ludwig IV, who, despite his title, had been excommunicated by the pope. The emperor, who theoretically ruled most of what is now Germany, although very loosely and vaguely had promised him help against Philippe for seven years and offered to make Edward vicar-general (or deputy) of the Empire. However, Edward had to bribe the Germans to join with £120,000 in payments, and so when he raised an army in 1337, the cost was already a staggering two hundred thousand pounds, several times his annual income.

In 1338, the French sacked Southampton; that year, Guernsey in the Channel Islands was also occupied, and the following year, the French raided the coast from Cornwall to Kent, attacking Dover and Folkestone and burning down much of the Isle of Wight. On March 23, 1339, Philippe had even issued an *ordonnance*—battle plan—for the full conquest of England, although he never carried it out. It was partly because of this terror and hatred of the French that the conflict was popular in England, and Edward was able to gather the support of the aristocracy, in particular the group of one hundred barons, bishops, and abbots who really mattered.[16] There was also a great deal of enthusiasm for invading France because, unlike Scotland, there was huge opportunity for theft.

Although most of the English warlords were from the landed aristocracy, there were scores of 'needy adventurers of obscure birth and no inherited property [who] made notable fortunes.'[17] The war offered many humble-born men the chance to come up in the world, most of them awful human beings and by today's standards war criminals. There was Sir John Chandos, a poor knight from Derbyshire, and Sir Thomas Dagworth, 'a bold professional soldier' who came from a middle-class Norfolk family, both of whom rose from obscurity to play a leading part in the war before dying horrifically violent deaths. John Hawkwood, the leader of the largest and most dangerous mercenary army, was the son of an Essex tanner.[18]

Edward's army was drawn from a 'commissions of array' and the commissioners—usually locals with military experience—were given the job of choosing men from their area to fight. Naturally the commissioners mostly picked the dregs of society who served no useful purpose back home, and it is estimated that 12 percent of Edward's army were outlaws, most of those murderers who could obtain a 'charter of pardon' if they fought. Many of the notorious gang members of the 1320s and 1330s ended up being pardoned and some even got knighthoods.

However, while he was in the Low Countries, Edward's supply of money dried up, which was not a good start. He blamed the lack of cash reaching him in Antwerp on treachery, and tried to stop the salaries of all officials and ministers until he was persuaded they would all resign if he did this. The problem was that the king had 'little understanding of the problems of taxation or credit and was bored by administration' and all his invasions were done on 'a hand-to-mouth basis, without budgets or forecasts.'[19] He just didn't understand that you couldn't fund wars in three different places at the same time, and despite Parliament voting in new taxes, Edward was already so broke that he left his pregnant wife Philippa in Ghent as security, as he could not pay the Flemish the money he promised them; while there, his wife gave birth to a son who therefore became known as John of Gaunt. The king told Parliament in the spring of 1340 that unless they raised more taxes he would be imprisoned for debt by the Flemish, which would probably be a bit humiliating.

In September 1339, Edward arrived in France with fifteen thousand men, including many German and Dutch mercenaries who were notorious at the time. Philippe, despite having thirty-five thousand men, didn't show up, leaving Edward with troops threatening to go home. This was the favored French tactic since they guessed the English would run out of money and food and become restless and leave. Edward, meanwhile, sent insulting letters to Philippe offering one-on-one combat, which the forty-seven-year-old was hardly likely to accept from a man twenty years younger, or alternatively to combat between one hundred of the best knights selected by each. The Frenchman did not take up his offer.

The first battle of the war took place in Sluys in Flanders, where the English defeated a navy twice as large and left so many of their enemy dead that it was said that if fish spoke, they could have learned French.

Sluys was a textbook case of French bureaucratic inflexibility. Their navy was led by a Genoese sailor with the suitably terrifying name Barbanera, or Blackbeard, and included Genoese war galleys with rams and catapults, but despite their advantage the French were, characteristically, hamstrung by a horror of anything that contradicted correct procedure in that charming way the French have. So Blackbeard had to ask permission of the two French leaders in charge, Hugues Quieret and Nicolas Behuchet, before doing anything despite the fact they weren't even sailors—Behuchet was a tax collector. So they stayed in anchor and when Edward arrived, the more powerful French ships were trapped.

In the course of the day, the English destroyed or captured 190 of 213 French boats, and some sixteen to eighteen thousand French soldiers and seamen died, as well as all of Philippe's admirals. A chronicler recorded: 'The sea was so full of corpses that those who did not drown could not tell whether they were swimming in water or blood, though the knights must have gone straight to the bottom in their heavy armor.' Blackbeard, seeing what a disaster it was, led his men away. The two French leaders surrendered, but Quieret was immediately beheaded and Buhechet was hanged after a few minutes and left on the galley to demoralize the French.

All throughout, Edward was in the thick of the fighting, getting blood splattered on his white leather boots. The battle ended with thirty French ships fleeing, with only one ship—the *Saint-Jacques of Dieppe*—continuing to fight into the night; when it was finally captured by the Earl of Huntingdon, four hundred corpses were found on board the ship.

The worst tragedy for the English occurred when one of their ships was sunk carrying 'a great number of countesses, ladies, knights' wives, and other damsels, that were going to see the Queen at Ghent' after being struck by cannon. Bizarrely, wives were quite often brought along to watch battles, 'health and safety' not really being a thing at the time.

Edward commemorated the victory by making a special gold coin worth six shillings and eight pence, which showed him on board a ship on the waves with a crown on his head and carrying an impressive sword and shield. This sort of propaganda went down very well at home, where there wasn't much reflection on the pity and horror of war.[20]

Afterward, no one wanted to tell King Philippe about the disaster so it was left to a jester.

'Our knights are far braver than the English,' he said.

'Why is that?' the king asked.

'Because the English don't dare to jump into the sea in full armor.'

However, despite this glorious victory, two years later the French were able to sack Plymouth again, and Edward soon had to give up in France as he was running out of money. He came back furious and convinced that it was all the fault of his ministers for not finding him enough money, blaming the chancellor and archbishop of Canterbury, John Stratford. Edward, bizarrely, told the pope that Stratford had deliberately kept the king short of money in the hope that he would be killed because he wanted to have sex with the queen. Stratford had to take sanctuary in Canterbury, terrified the monarch would have him executed.

In 1341, Edward was so broke that he couldn't repay his loans, including £180,000 borrowed from Florentine bankers. Because of him, in 1343, the Peruzzi family went bankrupt, still owing seventy-seven thousand pounds even before interest; the following year another powerful banking family, the Bardi, also went under.

However, soon another angry aristocrat turned up in England, a Norman knight called Geoffrey d'Harcourt who wanted the English to invade because the French king had given his beloved, one Jeanne Bacon, to a crony to marry. The knight, 'another volatile adventurer, a man of hopeless dreams rather like Robert of Artois,'[21] told Edward to come to Normandy because there was 'so much booty' and 'no one would resist.'

Edward couldn't refuse such a suggestion and he sailed for Normandy in June 1346 with fifteen thousand men including many of the usual riffraff. They arrived in Caen and when the people in the city saw the army approaching they fled in horror, falling over one another in their rush to escape. Which was wise, as after some of the locals had thrown rocks and metal from the rooftops at the invaders, Edward ordered for the entire town to be slaughtered and burnt; although d'Harcourt persuaded him that this might be a bit excessive, some three thousand were killed.

A new word entered the English language around this time, originally from Italian—*plunder*. After Caen was ransacked, the king 'sent into England his navy of ships charged with clothes, jewels, vessels of gold and silver, and other riches, and of prisoners more than 60 knights and 300 burgesses,' who would be ransomed. A chronicler called Thomas Walsingham wrote in 1348: 'there were few women who did not possess something from Caen, Calais or another town over the seas, such as clothing, furs and cushions. Tablecloths and linen were seen in everybody's houses. Married women were decked in the trimmings of French matrons and if the latter bemoaned their loss the former exulted in their gain.'

Unfortunately for the French, while in Caen, Edward found documentary proof of Philippe's 1339 *ordonnance*, and this made him even angrier. He ordered for copies to be made and read in every parish in England, including by the archbishop of Canterbury at St. Paul's so 'that he might thereby rouse the people.' To further his propaganda war, he also employed Dominican friars to go around from town to town explaining why the war was happening, a sort of fourteenth-century version of 'Why We Fight.' (The short answer: to steal tablecloths.)

Meanwhile, the Flemish poet Froissart became the king's chronicler; born in Hainault in 1337, he was described as 'the first war correspondent,' but he painted the king in a flattering manner.

After destroying Caen, the English headed in the direction of Paris, using the favorite tactic of the *chevauchée*, 'a rather glamorous term for what was essentially a traveling riot of looting, burning, rape, and murder.'[22] Its original meaning was a sort of horse ride or jaunt, but it came to mean going through an area and burning, stealing, and killing everything and everyone in sight, thereby forcing the local lord to fight. Edward wrote a letter to his eldest son, Edward the Black Prince, saying 'our people are burning and destroying to the breadth and depth 12 or 14 leagues of the country' and 'so that the country is quite laid waste of corn, of cattle and of any other goods.' He meant it as a good thing, like a progress report, rather than a lament about the woe of war—he also mentioned that the city of Cambrai in Flanders had been 'laid waste.' Good-o. (He did have some limits, however, and ordered that no church be attacked, hanging twenty of his men who had set fire to one in Beauvais.)

One English knight, Sir Geoffrey Scrope, took a French cardinal 'up a great and high tower, showing him the whole countryside towards Paris for a distance of fifteen miles burning in every place.'[23] He asked him, 'Sir, does it not seem to you that the silken thread encompassing France is broken?' and the cardinal collapsed. A yes, in other words.

After Caen, Edward's army of eight thousand men, half of them archers, marched through Normandy on their way to Paris. North of the capital they turned around to join their Flemish allies, and the French king trudged across the River Somme to catch them. The two sides met on August 13, 1346, at a place called Crecy-en-Ponthieu, where probably the greatest victory in English history was won.

CHAPTER SIX

Crecy

Half a century earlier, when the English had defeated the Welsh, they were so impressed with their enemies that they drafted them into their army. Even more than the soldiers, however, they were amazed with a Welsh invention, the longbow, which had a devastating effect on the French cavalry.

At the time, the most advanced weapon was the crossbow, which was considered so frightening when it was first introduced in the twelfth century that the Church tried banning its use. However, the new weapon, despite looking more primitive, could fire off up to twelve iron-tipped arrows a minute, compared to the crossbow's four, and its arrows were lethal at a range of 150 yards (while at sixty yards they could pierce plate armor). In the first minute at Crecy, the Anglo-Welsh archers fired seventy thousand arrows, each archer letting off his sixth missile before the first one had landed.

It took years of experience to get good at the longbow, which usually lead to chronic spine problems, and since Edward I's reign, such practice had been mandatory with 'every yokel being commanded by law to practice at the butts on Sunday.' Longshanks also banned football, as it distracted from archery, although the street violence associated with the sport also unnerved the authorities. The two constants of English life through the centuries are (1) heavy alcohol use, and (2) an inability to see a soccer ball without having a mass brawl, usually also involving constant (1). In France, meanwhile, owning a weapon was banned because it made the aristocracy nervous and, however much the English frightened them, they feared and despised their own peasants more.

A further act of 1369 also banned hockey, handball, cockfighting, and 'other such idle games' on pain of imprisonment, while another law decreed that if an archer killed a man while practicing then it should not be considered a crime. Up and down the country, young men larked about with arrows tipped with sharp steel that were able to penetrate an oak door four inches thick, at a time when the average person consumed eight pints of beer a day. What could go wrong?

Archers were well paid, especially mounted archers who got six pence a day, which was the same as a master craftsman; the foot archer received three pence, which compared well to a good plowman who made two pence. Mounted archers on ponies—who did not actually fire while mounted—were first used by Edward III in Scotland; a group from Cheshire would form a two hundred-strong royal bodyguard, all dressed in green and white uniforms. By 1346, the longbow was standardized with each archer carrying two-dozen arrows, backed by further supplies.

The longbow did much to undermine the class system because archers were so effective against mounted knights, who, because of the costs involved, had always been exclusively upper class. In the fourteenth century, plate armor—the full coats of armor that traditionally feature as comic props in stately homes in cartoons— replaced chain mail, which was of no use against direct sword attacks. The new material was incredibly heavy, dark, and stuffy inside, 'a terrible worm in an iron cocoon' as one former soldier described it, and men would often have heart attacks just walking around in the thing. It was also expensive, although horses were the biggest cost. The term 'man-at-arms' applied to those classes—knight-bannerets, knight-bachelors, and esquires—who could afford two armed valets and three mounts per men-at-arms, a warhorse, a packhorse for armor, and a palfrey (a cheap horse) to ride outside of battle. All of this required a fair bit of money as the giant warhorses of this period cost the huge sum of two hundred pounds (for that you could get a horse trained to bite opponents).

The war also saw the first use of firearms, although it was not until the very end of the conflict that they became hugely effective. In 1345, Edward ordered the making of one hundred ribaults, which fired twelve metal balls at high speed, but 'such weapons were seldom lethal, except to those firing them' although 'they produced plenty of noise, flame, and acrid black smoke.'[1]

The main weapon of both the French and English soldiers was a dagger called a *misericord* or mercy-killer, so-called as it usually finished off the fatally wounded; soldiers wore the dagger on the right with a long sword on their left, although the Welsh footmen wore long knives on the back of their belts, which some historians think added to the long-established myth that Englishmen had tails.

At Crecy, the French heavily outnumbered the English with fifteen thousand Genoese crossbowmen, twenty thousand men at arms, thousands of knights on horseback, and a lot more peasants. As well as their four thousand archers, the English had just two thousand foot soldiers and fifteen hundred knifemen. However, the French troops did not reach the battlefield until 4 p.m. when the sun was in their eyes; they were also tired after a long march, and their bowstrings were wet from a storm, while the English and Welsh had protected theirs by rolling them in their helmets. Had the French waited until morning they would probably have won.

Worried there would be a scramble to capture high-value opponents, at the start of the battle the French unfurled the *oriflamme* flag, signifying that there would be no prisoners. The king of England followed suit.

However, with a hail of English arrows the Genoese crossbowmen soon ran off, and after three courageous assaults, the French were caught in the mud, helpless as the arrows rained down. Afterward, Welsh knifemen were sent in after dark to sneak under the enemies' horses and cut open their stomachs, and then the Frenchmen above them.

Although King Edward was still barely in his midthirties, at an age many men today are still basically adolescents, alongside him in battle was his son Edward of Woodstock, known to history as the Black Prince because of his distinctive armor, who was aged just sixteen.[2] During the fight, he was knocked off his feet and left helpless in his mail, at which point the standard bearer Richard de Beaumont covered him with the banner of Wales and heroically protected him from being killed until he was able to get up. Although Froissart has a story about Edward refusing to help his son with the quote, 'Let the boy win his spurs for I want him, please God to have all the glory,' another contemporary, Geoffrey le Baker, says the king sent twenty knights to relieve his son—which seems more likely.

By the end of the day, fifteen hundred French noblemen and ten thousand of their regular soldiers lay dead. Among the fallen was fifty-year-old King John of faraway Bohemia, who wanted to get involved in the fighting despite being totally blind. Twelve of his best men chose to tie all their horses together so they could lead their king into battle and, rather unsurprisingly, all but two were killed— 'found the next day lying around their leader with their horses still fastened together.'

King John, who had lost his eyesight while on Crusade in Lithuania, was one of the more colorful figures in the war. In the words of one writer, he 'loved fighting for its own sake, not caring whether the conflict was important,' and in between wars he would enter tournaments.[3] Although most likely it was because of an infection, his subjects believed he was struck blind after digging up the tomb of Saint Adelbert in Prague Cathedral to get at money hidden there.

According to popular legend, so impressed was the Black Prince by this noble act of heroic stupidity that he took John's emblem of three ostrich feathers and the motto *Ich Dien*, German for 'I serve,' as his own, and today it is still the emblem of the Prince of Wales. Unfortunately, there's no evidence it's actually true.

Although the rain and sun didn't help, the French also lost because they were too busy showing off, as the whole aim of chivalry was to be at the center of the glory; little thought was given to actual tactics, and chaotic groups of horsemen were vulnerable to well-organized archers. The chivalric ideal was all about being flashy, such Victorian ideas as modesty and reticence being unknown, and even fashion reflected this; knights at this time wore *poulaines*, excessively long, pointed shoes that had to be tied up around the calf just so the person could walk, while Chaucer criticized the wearing of codpieces over trousers and the flaunting of 'shameful privee membres' by men that make it appear like they're suffering a hernia.

Philippe, whose brother Charles was among those killed, fled the scene at the end of the day and found a house where he asked the man to open up to 'the unfortunate king of France,' a pun on his nickname 'the fortunate.'

Crecy also saw the first use of cannon and gunpowder in Europe, which the French had acquired from Italy; originally used by the Chinese in the eighth century, this would change medieval Europe and its feudal system based around castles, impenetrable fortresses that could withstand rebellions or invading armies, but were useless against the new technology.

Around the same time, the English also won a victory over the Scots at Neville's Cross in Durham after King David II made the mistake of invading, which led to inevitable defeat. The king spent nine years in the Tower of London and, to make matters worse, the English also took back 'the Black Rood of Scotland,' supposedly a piece of Christ's Cross kept in a black case. The man who captured

King David, John de Coupland, received five hundred pounds a year for life, but was later murdered by jealous neighbors.

Edward still couldn't conquer Paris, so he marched around it and instead arrived at Calais, which the French had used as a base for raids on English wool ships, and besieged it with thirty thousand men. After the city was reduced to starvation, eventually five hundred of the weakest were sent out, but Edward refused to let them through the lines, and they were left to die. He then demanded everyone surrender, while Philippe withdrew and left the city to its fate; as his troops marched off, the people inside tore down the French coat of arms and threw it over the walls in disgust.

When a leading citizen said he was ready to surrender, Edward replied that the people would be ransomed or killed as in battle, but an English knight persuaded the king to execute just half a dozen leading citizens, sparing the rest. Six men volunteered, walking out of the city stripped to the waist with nooses around their necks. It was all very dramatic and eventually Edward was begrudgingly persuaded by his wife to spare them, allowing the six men to live 'with evident ill-grace.'[4] Queen Phillipa pleading with Edward for the burghers of Calais became a famous theme and was depicted first in a painting by Benjamin West and then on a Rodin sculpture in the city itself, with twelve copies of the sculpture at various spots around the world, including Westminster (by French law no more than twelve replicas can be made, because rules).[5]

After Edward took Calais, he gave each inhabitant a meal before expelling them, and set up an English colony there, part of the general policy that would be called ethnic cleansing today; Calais remained a rather strange outpost of England for another two hundred years, a huge drain on the treasury that the English insisted on keeping.

And the English almost lost the city straightaway. They put an Italian adventurer in charge and, in December 1349, the French bribed the new governor to open the gates to them—and if you can't trust an Italian adventurer who can you trust? Unfortunately, he double-crossed them, the gate was opened, the French leaders walked in, and then the gate shut behind them. On New Year's Eve, they were entertained to dinner by the king of England himself, 'bareheaded save for a chaplet of fine pearls.'

The Order of the Garter

After Calais, Edward went on a victory tour, starring in tournaments and taking in the adulation of the public. The king loved such show business events, which were also a good excuse to dress up; the previous year he had donned an 'exotic green animal outfit for both a joust in which he took part and for that year's Christmas festival at court.'[6]

In honor of his great victory, the king created an order of chivalry on April 23, 1348—St. George's Day. According to one theory, the Order of the Garter had begun as an in-joke between Edward and some of his oldest, most trusted friends, and the use of a garter may have been a bit of lighthearted sexist locker-room humor referencing their wild and carefree younger days. They were in their midthirties, so perhaps the order was the first manifestation of a midlife crisis; nowadays, they'd have just bought Porsches. It was also influenced by the Arthurian legend, which was now reaching its peak, the twenty-four knights of the Garter making up Edward's own Round Table.

It supposedly started in Eltham Palace in Kent, where the king was dancing or in some way was involved in a racy incident with Joan, Countess of Salisbury, said to be the greatest beauty of her age. They were probably lovers, although she was also his future daughter-in-law and ironically known as 'the maiden of Kent' because she was 'the most amorous' of women.

While dancing, the countess's garter slipped from her leg, revealing her stockings, and the room full of men erupted into sniggers. Edward picked up the lady's clothing and tied it around his own leg, exclaiming *Honisoit qui mal y pense* ('Shame on him who thinks evil of it'). Today, it is still the motto of the order, and appears on the masthead of royal crests, as well as in involved *The Times* of London newspaper.

Edward certainly had what used to be called an eye for the ladies, but despite this he had a successful marriage to Philippa of Hainault, with whom he had five sons and three daughters who grew to adulthood. Edward even let his eldest son choose his own wife, extremely unusual at the time, and the other children helped to seal alliances with leading baronial families. This may, however, have helped to ensure future conflict likely because so many leading clans had some claim to the throne.

In practical terms, the Order of the Garter was used as a form of meritocracy. Men who were not part of the actual elite were raised up so that they could be made useful without giving them lands or titles; one of Edward's first nominations was Roger Mortimer, grandson of the man he had killed at Tyburn, who had his land and honor restored after fighting at Crecy. (Of the original twenty-four Order of the Garter members, twenty had been at the battle and two others may have been, including the wonderfully named Sachet d'Abrichecourt.)

The order might have been the idea of Edward's cousin, Henry of Grosmont, Duke of Lancaster and nephew of his father's arch-nemesis. He was known as the 'Father of Soldiers' because he did not miss a battle in forty-five years; even when England was not at war, Lancaster had traveled around Europe looking for conflicts, fighting for Alfonso of Castile against the Moors at the siege of Algeciras in 1343, and in Prussia for the Teutonic Knights in their own Crusade against pagans. While in Spain, Henry would have seen the Order of the Band, Castile's brotherhood of knights, and taken the idea back. Afterward, King Jean of France was so impressed with the Garter that he began his own, the Order of the Star.

In 1352, after returning from Prussia, Lancaster challenged Duke Otto of Brunswick to combat and rode into court in Paris on horseback where he was given an enthusiastic welcome by French nobles, who, despite there being a war and everything, loved a bit of flamboyance. His opponent 'trembled so violently on his war-horse that he could not put on his helmet or wield his spear and had to be removed by his friends and retract his challenge.'[7] Afterward, Lancaster was offered a grand prize as his reward but accepted only a thorn from the 'saviour's crown,' a relic owned by the French king, which he returned home to put in his church in Leicester.[8]

Such was Lancaster's renown in battle that he had been promoted to duke in 1351, and went on to use all his plunder from France to build the Savoy Palace on the Strand, now the site of the famous hotel of the same name.

Chivalric fighting was so popular that there were sometimes tourneys between opposing sides during wars, which happened at Alnwick in 1327 between the English and Scots. During the Crecy campaign, a French knight challenged any comer to three jousts 'for the love of his lady.' An Englishman, Sir Thomas Colville, stepped forward; they fought two but a third fight had to be abandoned.

The same year as the Garter was founded, the king also adopted Saint George as the patron of England, capping off a remarkable rise to power for a saint who was not only foreign but also very obscure. According to tradition, he had been a Roman soldier martyred in the fourth century during the Diocletian persecution, possibly in Libya or Palestine, although the Catholic Church teaches that his acts are 'known only to God.'[9] During the Crusades, western soldiers adopted Saint George after he appeared to them at the siege of Antioch in 1098, and English troops began to ride with his red and white cross into battle.

As the cult became more popular, the method of George's tortured martyrdom became wildly inflated; originally impaled with nails, the story grew so that he was first broken on the wheel, then roasted, boiled and/or burned to death, beheaded, and crucified on a variety of differently shaped crosses, so that at one point the story went that he was brought back to life just so he could be tortured to death again. By another account, he was supposed to have spent seven years dying painfully during a quite fantastically heroic martyrdom. George also went through a process of Anglicization, so by the fourteenth century it was claimed he came from Coventry in the west midlands.

April 23 became a major day in the English calendar from the fourteenth to the seventeenth century, when the Reformation made such religious festivals unpopular; it then came back into fashion after the 1996 European soccer championship, and these days it is mostly marked by torturous newspaper think pieces about the meaning of English national identity. George is also patron saint of Germany, Hungary, Lithuania, Armenia, Ethiopia, Catalonia, farmers, butchers, skin diseases, and the Plague. Meanwhile, native saints such as Edward the Confessor, Alban, and Edmund all declined in importance, and the last two had to make do with having commuter towns named in their honor.

Knighthood wasn't all glamor, however, and knights were already evolving into a sort of modern middle class, the kind of people who do worthy public sector jobs. By the 1220s, county knights were appointed alongside professional lawyers as justices in charge of delivering people to jail, and, in Edward III's reign, many knights were becoming justices of the peace, local magistrates who these days have to deal with juvenile delinquents and suchlike. JPs were ordered to meet regularly in 'quarter sessions,' a system that lasted until the 1970s, and became the basis of local administration and justice, as the role of the upper-middle class evolved from being warrior to lawyer. Today, the Order of the Garter still consists of the monarch and twenty-four knights, and meets every third week of June for a suitably Ruritanian ceremony where they all dress up in quaint outfits, but it has a less military flavor; David Brewer, a former insurance broker, became its 1,008th member in 2016.

CHAPTER SEVEN

Plague

G unpowder, first used in Crecy, had come by way of Italy, which was far more advanced than France or England both in terms of technology and culture, already showing the signs of the cultural explosion of the following century. In 1305, Giotto had painted the Scrovegni chapel in Padua; Dante, living in Florence, had completed his *Divine Comedy* in 1320; while, in 1345, the first humanist, Petrarch, had discovered Cicero's letters, an event often credited with kick-starting the fifteenth-century Renaissance.

Although Florence was the center of this flowering of culture, Italy's most powerful city-states were Venice and Genoa, whose wealth was built on trade with the East. Among Genoa's numerous trading colonies was Caffa in the Black Sea, which, in 1346, was under assault by the Tartars, a steppes people from central Asia who had once terrorized Eastern Europe.[1]

During the siege of Caffa, the Tartar soldiers began coming down with a mysterious disease that caused them to cough up blood, grow repulsive boils on their groins, and die in agony. The illness soon killed huge numbers of Crimean Tartars, an improbably large figure of eighty-five thousand often given. 'Fatigued, stupefied, and amazed' by this new illness,[2] the Tartars called off the siege, but in an attempt to demoralize their enemies catapulted the dead bodies of the victims over the walls, unaware they had pioneered an early form of biological warfare. The Genoese chucked the corpses in the sea, but it was too late, and soon they were faced with an epidemic. Realizing they could not survive future Tartar attacks in such a weakened state, they traveled in their boats back to Italy. Which the people back home must have really appreciated.

When Christians first heard stories of a new deadly disease that afflicted the Middle East, they thought it was divine retribution against the Turks and Saracens for taking Christian land. This confidence in heavenly support didn't last long, however, and a year after the Caffa siege, Italians in London first heard rumors of people back home dropping dead in huge numbers. Plagues of one sort or another have been a feature of human existence since the first cities were built, and there had been seventy major epidemics in the previous seven centuries. Further back there was the plague of Athens in the fifth century BC and the Justinian Plague that hit after the fall of the Roman Empire. But this new disease, known later as the Black Death, would be worse than anything before or since.

Yersinia pestis, the bacterium that carried the bubonic plague, had been living on gerbils in Tibet for a while and was harmless to other species, but unstable climate conditions in the 1340s caused the disease to mutate. In its new deadly form, it first hit China, which had in the previous years already suffered a series of unimaginable disasters. There had been drought and famine in the Yangtze River region, and a huge earthquake in Ki-Ming-Chan, after which whole mountains collapsed creating a huge lake. Then in Tche province, some five million are said to have died from earthquakes and floods from 1337–1345. There was also the Mongol invasion.

Not that Europe was having a great time either, for even before the Plague arrived, Italy had endured a series of tragedies, so that even without the Plague it would have been an exceptionally awful period. During those grim times, there were earthquakes in Naples,

Rome, Pisa, Bologna, Padua, and Venice; in July 1345, there was six months of rain that ruined crops followed by famine in 1346 and 1347. On top of this, there were a series of banking collapses, workers' riots in many cities, and also a terrible earthquake in January 1348 that destroyed whole villages.

As the year 1347 went on, more and more stories began to circulate in England of terrible things happening abroad; merchants who traded with Bordeaux heard that France was now infected. The following summer, on June 23, 1348—St. John's Eve, a flirting and fertility festival, the only day of the year when unmarried women could act in a risqué manner by dancing with men—a ship carrying the disease turned up in Melcombe in Dorset. Within a decade, England had lost between a third and half of its population.

The Rootless Phantom

The first sign of the dreaded illness was bad breath, though at the time most oral hygiene probably wasn't at the highest standard to begin with. Then the afflicted suffered huge black growths on their armpits and groins before being struck down by a fever. Most victims would have four or five days of agonizing pain, after which between 60 and 90 percent would die.

To make matters more confusing to people with a limited knowledge of medical science, the disease came in three different forms, each of them ghastly although slightly different. The most common was bubonic plague, in which tumors the size of apples—inflamed lymphatic glands known as bubo—appeared on the neck, armpits, and groin, after which you were gone within a week.

Bubonic plague was transmitted by flea bites; the second type, pneumonic, spread through the air and contracted by breathing, was much more contagious and killed within forty-eight hours; in the Manchurian epidemic of 1921, life expectancy for people with pneumonic plague was 1.8 days. Then there was the septicaemic version, which took place when bubonic and pneumonic plague infected the blood and led to internal hemorrhaging. This caused dark blotches across the body known as 'God's tokens,' and killed even more quickly, often within hours, although it was much less common. The Florentine poet Boccaccio wrote: 'How many brave men, how many fair ladies, how many gallant youths, whom any physician, were he Galen, Hippocrates or Aesculapius himself, would have pronounced in the soundest of health, broke fast with their kinfolk, comrades and friends in the morning, and when evening came, supped with their forefathers in the other world!' Simon of Covino wrote of priests who 'were seized by the [P]lague whilst administering spiritual aid; and, often by a single touch, or a single breath of the Plague-stricken, perished even before the sick person they had come to assist.'

The disease also caused intoxication of the nervous system, which led to depression and a sort of madness, just to add to the general apocalyptic air. According to *The Black Death* author Philip Ziegler: 'In Provence a man climbed on to the roof of his house and threw down the tiles into the street. Another executed a mad, grotesque dance on the roof.'[3]

People who were infected developed blood that was black and thick, and sometimes 'thin green scum' rose to the surface, which usually suggested the end was near: 'Everything that issued from body, breath, sweat, blood from lungs and boils, bloody urine and bloody feces—smelled foul' and after a while 'death is seen seated on the face.'[4]

'Many died of boils and abscesses, and pustules on their legs and under their armpits; others frantic with pain in their head, and others spitting blood,' wrote an Irish friar unfortunate enough to live at the time.

Over the course of 1349, the Plague spread across England, averaging a mile a day, and the death rates were apocalyptic in parts. Jarrow in County Durham, for instance, lost 80 percent of its population, but this was not by any means the worst. In the manor of Wakefield, it was recorded that the village of Shelf 'is dead,' while at the abbot of Eynsham's manor of Tilgarsely in 1359, it was reported that they couldn't raise tax in the village because it had been empty since 1350, and this was not a small or poor settlement beforehand. In Cuxham in Oxfordshire, every one of twelve tenant farmers died in 1349, and four of eight cottagers. In Winchester, six parish churches were abandoned. The Plague led to ghost villages—some three thousand in England—although many were killed off not just by the actual disease but by peasants fleeing for better wages that followed, while in others there were clearances afterward as unprofitable humans were replaced by sheep.

With churchyards unable to cope, huge plague pits were built;[5] sometimes the living were thrown in with the dead, and the piles of corpses were seen to squirm from the movements of the dying. Mass burials had to be carried out with not enough living to bury the dead, while many also abandoned bodies, or dying family members, so terrified were they of the disease.

Over 1348–9, half of London's fifty thousand people died, while the death toll in Paris was up to eighty thousand out of a population of 150,000. When a village became infected, a black flag was flown over the parish church, and there were often so many corpses that church graveyards would stink from a great distance. The Plague was likened to 'black smoke' or a 'rootless phantom,'[6] and many quite reasonably thought it was the end of the world.

King Edward was asked to stay in the city of London to help with morale; his exact reply has never been recorded, but it was something to the effect of 'get stuffed.' However, even the royal family was affected by the disease: the king's daughter Joanne died of it on her way to Castile to marry Pedro the Cruel, although as he ended up later murdering his wife, perhaps she dodged a bullet.

Desperate for some divine help, the monarch wrote to Archbishop of Canterbury John Stratford in September 1348, asking him to put together some special national prayers. Unfortunately, as it turned out, the archbishop had died of the Plague over a week earlier. His successor, John de Ufford, lasted just six months before also succumbing to the pestilence; after him came Thomas Brad-wardine, who perished from the disease within six weeks.

For a very few people, however, the Plague was a stroke of luck. At Eynsham Abbey in Oxfordshire, Abbot Nicholas was deprived of his office for some unrecorded wrongdoing. Bishop Gynewell nominated two administrators to run the abbey before a new man could be found, but they soon both died, and so the two monks who brought the news were given their jobs instead. However, both men were dead before they even reached the Abbey, and so Abbot Nich-olas got the job back.

The Scots mockingly called the disease 'the foul death of England . . . God's judgment on the English' and seeing that their neighbor was weakened, they decided to invade in 1349, with pre-dictable results. Their forces amassed in Selkirk, 'laughing at their enemies,' and were about to swarm across the border when 'the fearful mortality fell upon them and the Scots were scattered by sudden and savage death so that, within a short period, some five thousand died.'[7] The soldiers went home, dying on the road and spreading the disease to their homes, as they lamented from the 'foule deth that Ynglessh men dyene upon.'

In Ireland, Friar John Clyn of Kilkenny described rather gloomily, 'waiting among the dead for the coming of death. I have committed to writing those things that I have truly heard and seen, and lest the work of recording perish together with the writer, I leave parchment just in case any human survivor should remain who might wish to continue the work that I have begun.' He died soon after, rather justified in his pessimism.

Almost everywhere in Europe the same story was repeated, although Italy was the worst affected with maybe two-thirds of the population wiped out. Gherado, brother of the famous poet Petrarch, was one of thirty-six members of a Carthusian monas-tery at the onset of the Plague—and the only one left afterwards.

Every day he buried as many as three of his fellow monks 'until he was left alone with his dog and fled to look for a place that would take him in.'

Because of the Plague, Siena Cathedral, which would have been the most enormous in the world, was never finished, although it looks fairly spectacular as it is. Florence was the worst affected with well over half of its population killed; its great historian Giovannni Villani died in mid-sentence, writing 'in the midst of this pestilence there came to an end . . . ' before succumbing.

The period was also marked by a number of other freakish disasters, which reinforced the idea that someone up there didn't like them. A tidal wave destroyed much of Cyprus and despite the people trying to flee to the hills, 'a pestiferous wind spread so poisonous an odour that many, being overpowered by it, fell down suddenly and expired in dreadful agonies.'[8]

In some parts of Europe, such as Dubrovnik, wolves walked into towns and ate corpses openly; in others, the animals shied away from humans, fearful of their disease.

Scandinavia was infected via England; it was brought to Norway by a ship in May 1349, in which someone had come aboard already ill and while at sea the whole crew died. The empty boat drifted toward Bergen like a scene straight from a Werner Herzog film, the unsuspecting locals going aboard before they realized what had killed the passengers.[9] Some Swedes fled from civilization in order to build a mountain hideaway in a new town called Tusededal, but the Plague followed, and from their sanctuary just one girl survived, discovered years later and shunning human company. She was christened Rype, or 'wild bird,' but eventually returned to normal and married; in fact her family, the Rypes, were still big land owners in the area centuries later.

In Avignon, where the papacy had been situated since 1309, one graveyard received eleven thousand corpses in six weeks, and so many people died that the pope had the Rhone River consecrated so people could just chuck the bodies in without worrying about their souls.

Not every region suffered equally; Bohemia and Poland were almost entirely unaffected, partly because the king of Poland had closed the border but also because that part of Europe was off the beaten track. Milan had a far lower death rate than most cities because its exceptionally cruel ruler Luchino Visconti (later poisoned by his wife) acted with ruthless efficiency: when the disease was first discovered, all the occupants of the three houses affected were walled up and left to die. The Duke of Milan also decreed anyone who brought the Plague into the city was subject to the death penalty, which seems a bit unnecessary; Plague victims were otherwise taken out of the city to die or recover in the fields. Meanwhile, in Venice, beggars were banned from displaying corpses in the streets, 'as was their macabre custom.'

Generally, people in the cities had a far higher death rate due to greater human contact but also because of the squalor. The population of England had tripled since the Norman Conquest, and this led to filthy, overcrowded towns filled with rat-friendly wood and straw buildings. As one author put it: 'The medieval house might have been built to specifications approved by a rodent council as eminently suitable for the rat's enjoyment of a healthy and carefree life.'[10]

Cities really were disgusting most of the time; in 1307, the Palace of Westminster had a pipe that carried waste out through a sewer but this was probably unique, and most excrement was just thrown into a ditch or the street. The River Fleet, a tributary of the Thames to the west of London, was so choked by the filth from eleven latrines and three sewers that parts of it did not flow due to the buildup. In London, rakers occasionally threw the city's filth into great pits outside the city or in the river, but that was about the extent of sanitary policy, while the streets were filled with rotting animal heads, offal, and fish.

London was so disgusting people would pipe their waste into the unused cellars of unsuspecting neighbors, as the Assize of Nuisances discovered in 1347 when one such basement overflowed; or they dug cesspools in their yards and constructed DIY latrines. One fourteenth-century Londoner, Roger the Raker, did this so often that the pit filled to capacity and began to rot the floorboards, and on one visit he unfortunately plunged through the floorboards and drowned in his own excrement. Probably not how he envisioned his life turning out. Sewage and drinking water were often in close proximity with obviously negative results, and tanners' and dyers' waste also went into the water supply. It was little wonder that people chose to drink alcohol instead.

In 1300, Edward I had ordered the people of Oxford to clean up their town because, he complained, 'the air is so corrupted and infected that an abominable loathing [is] diffused among the foresaid masters and scholars.' His grandson would introduce rules about hygiene in London, restricting certain activities in the city, and banishing trades to outposts such as Knightsbridge. And progress was being made: public latrines were in London and in a handful of other cities, and fresh water pipes were also in London, Exeter, Southampton, and Bristol.

Health at the time was not great anyway. Lots of people had skin diseases, for example, and eye infections were also common; animals lived with people, and clothes were rarely washed. Remains of Plague victims in London showed that many had suffered from malnutrition and around one in six had rickets—the bone disease caused by lack of vitamins—a problem that had increased in previous centuries due to population pressure.

Across Western Europe, the previous population boom was now reversed, and many areas would not recover their pre-Plague levels until centuries later.[11] When Kenneth Clark went to film the BBC2 television series *Civilisation* in Sienna, he was told the population was less than its pre-Plague levels by two people.

Theories

In October 1348, the king of France asked the leading thinkers at the University of Paris for their theories about what was causing the disease. Putting together all their knowledge, wisdom, and studies, the doctors concluded that it was all down to 'a triple conjunction of Saturn, Jupiter, and Mars in the 40th degree of Aquarius' that took place on March 20, 1345, because a conjunction of Saturn and Jupiter always brought disaster and Mars and Jupiter together meant plague. Well it's a theory, and it became the official explanation accepted across the continent, even in Muslim Spain.[12]

Medical science had hardly improved since classical Greece; surgery was also seen as low-grade manual labor, and touching naked bodies was viewed as beneath the dignity of a cleric; this is why surgeons in Britain are today not doctors but mere misters. The most important anatomist of the age, John of Ardene, who 'made important contributions to the treatment of gout, clysters, and fistula,' learned everything from being an army surgeon in the Hundred Years' War, where the one thing they weren't short of was dead bodies.[13]

Across Europe it was believed that 'bad drove out bad' so people took to inhaling unpleasant odors to rid themselves of the horrible-smelling plague. Contemporary doctor John Colle believed that '[a]ttendants who take care of latrines and those who serve in hospitals and other malodorous places are nearly all to be considered immune.' As a result, 'it was not unknown for apprehensive citizens of a plague-struck city to spend hours each day crouched over a latrine absorbing with relish the foetid smells.'[14]

Other remedies, in the words of one historian, 'have a certain antiquarian charm but you would not want to undergo them.'[15] A handbook for doctors at St. Bart's in London recommended women's milk sucked directly from the breast, and if no lactating women were available then asses' or goats' milk should work. How the women felt about having Plague victims fondling their breasts is never explained; the donkeys probably weren't that ecstatic either, for that matter. Also advised was having a bath with the head entirely covered and chest wrapped in the skin of a small goat, which probably couldn't do much harm.

It wasn't until the nineteenth century that humans learned the cause of bubonic plague—rats and their plague-carrying fleas—and it's quite reasonable to be confused, as the disease-carrying fleas could survive forty days without a rat.

Whatever the fancy theories of the eggheads at Paris University, most people thought the obvious answer was that the 'Great Mortality,' as they called it, was caused by God's anger. Contemporaries saw all sorts of omens to confirm this: a column of fire was spotted above the papal palace at Avignon, a ball of flames above Paris, a stranded whale, mysterious bloodstains on men's clothes that turned out to be butterfly excrement. There was a small earthquake in Hull in December 1348, followed by the birth of conjoined twins nearby.

The pope decreed that a penitent procession be held in which many people would meet to atone for their sins, with groups of up to two thousand getting together, the unfortunate but predictable result being that a lot of them got the Plague.

Inevitably, many blamed the disaster on loose morals, and such abominations as men dressing in sexually provocative clothes, so that 'from the back the wearers look more like women than men.' Others attacked bodily adornments, such as full doublets 'cutted on the buttok,' which 'inflame women with lecherous desires.' They also looked at such manifestations of decadence as tournaments, where women were dressed in 'the most sumptuous male costumes,' tight trouser-wearing female cheerleaders at jousts seen as indicative of Edward III's dubious morals.

The misanthropic chronicler Henry Knighton wrote that they 'wearied their bodies with fooleries and wanton buffoonery . . . But God, in this matter, as in all others, brought marvellous remedy.'

Knighton, it's fair to say, was pretty reactionary even by the standards of the day, and most people thought God had gone too far this time.

Much of the new fashion for racier, more sexualized clothing came down to a simple thirteenth-century invention, the button, which allowed clothes to be more figure-hugging and therefore emphasize masculine or feminine body parts.

Across the water, John of Bridlington blamed the Plague on the king of France and his 'avarice, luxury, envy, gluttony, and anger,' which in fairness was an accurate description of his personality. King Philippe responded to the disease with laws against blasphemy; for the first offense a man would lose a lip, for the second the other lip, and for the third the tongue. London guilds also banned apprentices from cutting their hair 'like a gallant or a man of court,' while the Siena city council banned gambling 'forever' in June 1348, although this led to such a loss of revenue that 'forever' turned out to be 'until the end of the year.' Dice across Italy were banned and so dice makers instead moved to selling religious knickknacks.

Morality laws were also introduced in the city of Tournai in Flanders, so men and women living together were ordered to marry at once. Swearing, playing dice, and working on Sundays were all banned; no bells were to be rung at funerals, no mourning clothes worn, and no wakes held.

The strangest consequence of the Black Death was the rise of the Flagellant movement, in which groups of hundreds of people moved from town to town dressed in sackcloth and whipped themselves. The Brotherhood of the Cross, as the movement was called, seemed to emerge spontaneously and involved large groups of men stripped to the waist, 'scourging themselves with leather whips tipped with iron spikes until they bled.'[16] They cried out 'Spare us!' to God and Christ and the people cried in sympathy; they'd do three times a day, and it would go on for thirty-three and a half days to symbolize Christ's time on earth. Members weren't allowed to wash, shave, talk, change their clothes, or sleep in bed without their master's permission, and they were also supposed to adopt celibacy, although they were also accused of having orgies.

Collective self-harming sessions would start with each member rhythmically beating their chests and backs with a scourge, an instrument that had three or four metal-studded leather thongs attached, all the while being cheered on by a crowd and their master. The onlookers would encourage them by singing the Hymn of the Flagellants, until eventually the fanatical self-harmers would throw themselves to the ground before reaching a crescendo of mortification.

This insanity swept through Germany, the Low Countries, and Northern France, becoming larger and increasingly hysterical until, inevitably, they became violent, in particular against the Catholic hierarchy. Church leaders tried to stop the group but whenever priests got in their way they were assaulted or killed. Some Flagellants came to London in 1349, whipping themselves outside St. Paul's—where they were received with stony silence by the mystified English who presumably just found the whole thing so embarrassing.

It came amid an atmosphere of increased hostility toward authority generally, but the mob soon moved on to a more obvious target, and soon an epidemic of anti-Semitic pogroms swept across Europe. At first, people blamed lepers for the Plague, and victims of the disease were banned from entering the city of London because they were accused of trying to 'contaminate others with that abominable blemish' through 'their polluted breath, as by carnal intercourse with women in stews and other secret places.' Lepers had always been the object of suspicion, and, in 1321 in Languedoc, all the lepers were accused of poisoning wells, bribed to do so by the Jews on behalf of the Muslim king of Granada. Why or how these three totally disparate, random groups could have gotten together to hatch this scheme no one thought to properly explain.

But people believed some quite outlandish theories. One Polish historian, Dlugoss, thought the Jews had managed to poison the air with Plague, while many thought Jews were working for the leader of Muslim Spain, and that powdered poison was imported in large quantities from the East. However, the main conspiracy theory involved Jews poisoning the water supply.

Suspicion was partly aroused because Jews often did drink from open streams rather than from dirty wells, as Jewish ideas about hygiene were a bit further advanced due to their religious rules. A Swiss chronicler noted that Jews knew wells to be full of 'bad, noxious moistures and vapours' and there were even recorded incidences of them warning gentile neighbors to avoid the wells because they were so filthy, for all the thanks they got.

The first big massacres took place in Languedoc in the south of France, followed by Strasbourg where two thousand people were killed in a riot, with pogroms on a scale that would not be seen again until the twentieth century. The pope denounced the persecution and repeatedly attacked the rumors, pointing out that Jews were dying in large numbers from the disease, too, but the mob could not be controlled.

Only in England was there no massacre of the Jews, mainly because there were none left after Edward I had persecuted them.[17]

Social Impact

Whether or not loose morals had caused the Plague, they were certainly a result of it, as people reasoned that if they were going to die soon of a horrific disease they may as well have fun now. Churchman William Dene of Rochester complained that 'the entire population, or the greater part of it, has become even more depraved, even more prone to every kind of vice, more readily to indulge in evil and sinfulness, without a thought of death.' Another contemporary, John Gower, wrote a miserable book called *Vox Clamantis*, 'The Voice of One Crying Out,' in which 'he described how man grew increasingly feckless, corrupt and base, turning from God, obsessed by material gain, and ripe for divine punishment.'[18]